ALL THINGS EDIBLE, RANDOM AND ODD

Essays on Grief, Love, and Food

SHEILA SQUILLANTE

NON-FICTION

NON-FICTION

For my parents, Richard Squillante (1945-1992) and Eileen Kelly (1949-2021); my children, Rudy and Josephine; and for my husband, Paul—with love and gratitude for every shared morsel, the bitter and the sweet.

CONTENTS

ALL THINGS EDIBLE,
RANDOM AND ODD

I am trying to write about food and my relationship with my father and I keep writing variations of the phrase, "My father died almost eighteen years ago." Why do I prefer this phrasing to "My father has been dead almost eighteen years?" Something active about the revision. Something alive: My father *died*. Even in that ending he was acting. To be dead is to be passive, acted upon by dirt and time. I am mostly fine telling people that my father *died* but I find every day, even eighteen years later, that I am still not ready for my father to be *dead*.

When I was twelve years old, I found my grandmother sobbing in her bedroom. It scared me—she was a woman of exquisite restraint and composure—and I asked her what was wrong. "I miss your grandfather," she said. *Oh*, I thought, *is that all?* I was relieved but confounded: my grandfather had died when I was eighteen months old. My only connection to him were some pictures of him holding me as a newborn and a pair of patent-leather baby shoes in which, a month before he died, my grandfather drew a small, crooked smiley face in blue ballpoint pen, and scrawled, "Dear Sheila, this was the nicest gift I got. I love you. Grandpa." When I hold them now, nearly 40 years later, I can almost feel the way his hand shook as he wrote—all the love and fear, all the tension and energy of living and dying inscribed on the dingy white insole.

Apart from the shoes, which I treasure, I have nothing tangible to remind me, no memories of him at all. I recall wondering how my grandmother could be that upset over something that had happened so long ago. I was foolish. Of course, my grandfather's death was not a "something" but a "someone." I was a child the day my grandmother sobbed quietly in her bedroom over the man with whom she had lived for 28 years, the man with whom she had conceived twelve children, the man who had mourned with her the one child who died nine days after he was born. To me, my grandfather was much the same as the pictures in my father's *National Geographic* magazines of WWI soldiers or Chinese emperors of the Ming Dynasty. He was part of the Society of the Long Dead. But to my grandmother, his absence on that day was as near and real to her as it had been the day he died.

I understand this now. I know what it is to glance backward at five years or twelve years or more and see the landscape blur as it does from the window of a speeding car. To see it go that fast. I know how easy it is to conjure the dead, the past, the love, the skin, the warm smell of a man in a V-neck sweater. I am doing it right now; I cannot stop. I see him sitting cross-legged in a woven lawn chair in summer, drinking cold beer, eating deep-fried banana peppers and sweating from sun and spice. There he is pouring a second cup of coffee kissed with cinnamon from the pot I brewed for him. I am shaking through each of these sentences, stopping to remove my glasses and press my eyes so I won't cry in this public place where I am trying to write, where Aretha Franklin, Sam Cooke and Jackie Wilson are playing from the speakers. I pause, listen, and think: *my father loved this music.*

My father's picture hangs on what my husband and I jokingly call The Wall of Death in our home—a crisp and clear picture of a man whose very smell I can still recall, whose sensual essence lives on in me, in the rituals I've created, the tastes I savor, the meals I cook to honor and sustain him. But who is he to my four-year-old son and my two-year-old daughter but another member of that Society of the Long Dead? Quantifiable as fact. Static as biography. As dead as emperors and soldiers and great-grandfathers? Deader than dead. As dead as dead can be.

He died thirteen years before my son, who inherited his huge blue eyes, was even born. I try to tell him and his sister about their grandfather. I point out his pictures and tell them stories I think will charm them, make them laugh. "Your grandpa had a sweet tooth. He used to hide tins of Danish butter cookies under his bed, but we always found them. And once he ate a plateful of Christmas cookies before realizing they had been painted with Elmer's Glue to use as ornaments on the tree. He laughed when we told him, said they were the best cookies he had ever tasted!"

They are so young still and hardly understand what it means to live, let alone what it means to die. I want them to learn from their grandfather's catholic palate, his delight in discovering some new fruit in the grocery store or an unusual preparation at a restaurant. I cherish this side of my father—this fully sensual, fully present, wholly animal element. But I know I can't give my children the actual meals I had with him in white-clothed dining rooms and grubby pizza joints. They will never feel his hand reaching behind the front seat of the car to squeeze their knees, the way he did to my sister and me. But I have to give them something.

So, I want my essays to be horned melon and star fruit plucked from the produce aisle, salt-dough ornaments on a live tree sprinkled with white lights. Polished patent-leather and a message written in steady blue ink. Something they can hold in their hands. Something they can see and touch and feel.

I want to write about the meals my father and I shared because they were the glue that held our relationship together and because I have, in the eighteen years since he died, become the foodie that he was. In the last years of his life, my father had traveled all over the world for his job with IBM, bringing back ornately costumed dolls for my sister and me, and a taste for global cuisine.

I remember so much about the food itself. The way, for instance, the air in the first Indian restaurant he ever took me to was so redolent of curry and cardamom that my hair was perfumed by it hours after the meal had ended. I could write that scene now with little effort, describing a nineteen-year-old's thrill of anticipation and slight terror at this new, strange food.

I could describe my mother's hearty and delicious roasted chickens, baked zitis, and green bean casseroles laid out on the solid oak dining table in our blue-curtained kitchen, and then paint a contrasting image of the red and gold tapestries, the jeweled portraits of Hindu gods and goddesses that hung on the wall next to that restaurant table, how they glittered and swayed lightly every time the door opened to admit another hungry patron. I could talk about how the word "exotic" was the one playing over and over again in my mind as we ate crispy papadums and spicy chana dal cooled with raita.

I could even reflect studiously on my younger self, the one new to world cuisine, and observe that the perfumed air was actually heavy with oil and, in truth, quite difficult to breathe. Not, perhaps, the mark of an excellent restaurant. I could critique the ethnocentrism, the racism, even, embedded in my reliance on that word, "exotic." I could be that self-aware. My problem is not in remembering the food or the senses surrounding it. It is in remembering my father as a narrative *whole*.

Last night in bed, I said to my husband, "I don't have a very good memory." I was recounting a conversation I had had earlier that day with a girlfriend in which we shared stories of some of the more difficult parts of our growing up—relationship stories about who did what to whom and when. As she was describing the current situation between her and her mother-in-law, it was clear that she was building her narrative, and thus my ability to follow and understand it, upon details she had shared with me previously.

"I remember the first conversations," I told my husband, "and I have a sort of diffuse sense that there is some trouble in that relationship, but no matter how I try, I cannot recall the specifics. The details are lost to me."

"That's just a different kind of memory," he countered. "You remember so much about the way things tasted or felt or about the quality of sunlight on a particular day in mid-summer. Maybe what you have is a sensory memory."

Yes, maybe. But I have been worrying that a sensory memory is not a complete enough memory to accomplish the task of memoir. Whole conversations that I know my father and I had are more than murky. I can see us sitting in his car outside of my college dorm the warm spring day I had to leave, sobbing and ashamed, my suite full of girlfriends and get a "psychiatric single room" in a dorm on the far side of campus. I remember the feel of the black felted seats under my worrying fingers, and an overwhelming, surprising sense that he understood the exact shape and depth of my pain. But what did we say? Add to this the fact that my father was a terse, quiet man who largely kept his mouth closed unless he had something "important" to say, and what's left is, at best, a silhouette, a profile, a shadow. I want his words to fill the picture in and they are precisely what I don't have.

I began writing about my father at the beginning of my senior year of college, three weeks after his funeral on that blue-sky August day, and I spent that semester wandering around campus in a fog, sometimes making it to class, oftentimes opting to stay curled under blankets on the bed in my dorm room. I skipped so many classes in one course that by rights I shouldn't have been allowed to pass it or graduate. Only the compassion of my professors and poetry buoyed me through. I wrote and wrote that year, a series of poems documenting the ten days my 46-year-old father spent in ICU with a rare brain illness before we turned off life support. They were savage things, pulsing with pain and confusion and anger. It was the sort of project I now steer my own students away from, cautioning them against writing while still so close to the locus of their grief. But my thesis advisor, a man who introduced me to the poetry of Anne Sexton, Robert Lowell and Sylvia Plath —poetry that dwelled in the body and all its rough textures —knew that I needed to immerse myself. Embrace grief. Ingest it in order to survive it.

When I was in elementary school, our family moved from Kentucky to New Jersey. I was so bereft at leaving my friends that I forced myself to recite their names every day, convinced that as long as I could say them out loud, I would remember them. It was the same principle: as long as I could conjure every wrenching detail of my father's dying, as long as I could put myself back inside it, I would be able to keep him with me.

In graduate school ten years later, I was still writing about his dying, only now with more distance and, I hoped, more art. I was the Woman Who Wrote About Her Father in workshop. In three years, I don't think I made more than a handful of poems that didn't spring straight from those ten days I spent in the ICU waiting room, waiting for my father's body to shut down. I was trying to capture him in words and I was failing. The poems kept trying to define and classify. They made sweeping statements about loss that I thought I believed in before closing themselves up into neat little packages of still-raw pain. I could not see their artifice until an astute professor asked me, carefully, "Do you really want to keep your father inside a poem?"

No. I write because I want to *continue* my father, not contain him. I write about eating with him to delay his induction into my grandfather's dusty club, to keep him vital for myself and for my children. Because nothing is more open-ended than food. No matter how much we eat, we must keep eating. We will never, in this life, be sated.

In writing, I had almost convinced myself that the gaps in my memory, the silences between us, would mean my ultimate failure. I thought I needed his words to preserve him, but my father used words—spoken and swallowed—to keep all of us at a careful remove. To recall his words would be to recall a sound bite, a masterfully written script. An echo.

With each year that passes, I get that much closer to living longer than he did. He fades in and out like an erratic radio transmission, mostly weak and far away, but sometimes sharp and clear and nearer to me than my own voice.

When I cook and when I eat, I can hear my father—the self-made foodie who loved, as I once wrote in a poem, "all things edible, random and odd." He speaks his signature superlative, "Tremendous," while his thin fingers hold salmon sushi glistening between wooden chopsticks. I can taste turtle soup swirled with sherry from a crystal cruet and seaweed culled from the beach outside our hotel in Hawaii—how it popped in our mouths like fish eggs, rolling like excitement over our tongues.

I can also remember his blue eyes shot with red from years of avoiding his glasses and the deep scars on his leg where a dog mauled him as a child. I can remember his arm thrown hard against my chest as he braked the car in front of a motorcycle accident, Jackie Wilson crooning as we passed the wreck. I can remember his preference for women with faces scrubbed of makeup and barber-short hair, and his penchant for wearing soft V-neck sweaters, jeans and brown leather deck shoes. I can remember what he smelled like—*'Lectric Shave* and cigarette smoke. Peppermints and cardamom and curry.

I can remember. I will. I do.

MEAT RAGU

Serves 8-10 Country & Western lovers

For Ragu
1 lb hot or sweet Italian sausage
1 lb beef short ribs (salted and peppered generously)
6 large carrots, finely chopped
2 28 oz cans tomato puree
1 28 oz can water
2 medium onions, diced
3 large cloves garlic
½ cup chopped fresh parsley
3 tbsp fresh thyme
Salt & pepper to taste
1 tbsp olive oil
1 tbsp tomato paste
½ cup dry red wine

For Meatballs
1 lb ground beef
½ cup breadcrumbs
1 tbsp Dijon mustard

1 tsp tomato paste
¼ cup fresh chopped parsley
1 tsp dried basil
1 tsp dried oregano
1 clove fresh garlic, minced or pressed
¼ cup parmesan cheese
1 egg
½ cup milk
Salt & pepper

Begin near tears. This writing about your father is hard and you are an easy crier in the best of circumstances. You're making it harder on yourself, you realize, by choosing to play Waylon Jennings and Willie Nelson, whose music takes you right back to your father and your grandfather, your childhood, your great-grandmother Lucia's house (her meatballs, which you will not attempt!) on Sundays in White Plains, New York. *Sheila, you a nice-a girl, but you godda find a nice-a boy-a, settle down an getta married...*

This music might seem incongruous to the meal you are preparing—you are not Texan, not Southern in any way, your five years in Kentucky notwithstanding—but never mind and listen: Waylon and Willie and their kind await you back in Luckenback, Texas.

You are surrounded by nice boys today. Here in your home, your husband and son in and out of the back door, back and forth to the garden to gather your thyme and parsley. Waylon and Willie streaming on your laptop. Your father and your grandfather sitting poised, as if in a Country Western song, on adjacent tear drops, ready to spill. Plus, two more boys you're sharing this meal with: your friend, Dave, and his son, Ben. Dave is the one who gave you the idea for these recipe-essays, the key, you told him, to keep writing about your father. You are beyond grateful and he is fun to cook for. Appreciative and enthusiastic. *Affirming.* That one word, in fact, pretty much describes your whole friendship with Dave. It's hard to make friends in your 40's but here you are and aren't you lucky. You love to feed people—friends—so you will cook this ragu here in your own chaotic kitchen and then pack it into the car with your husband and kids and head over for a play/dinner date at 4PM. It's 11 am now. You'd better get this thing going as it's going to need long, slow heat.

"Luckenback Texas" is subtitled, "Back to the Basics of Love." It's about wanting to simplify, wanting to reconnect with someone you love. This is something your father might have been realizing, might have been working on when he died. Be thankful for that. Happy for him.

Chop your veggies first. Carrots from the farmer's market, their bushy green tops still attached. Onions, garlic, parsley, thyme. Your son wants to help, so put him in front of a bowl on the kitchen floor. Teach him how to thumb the thyme, stripping the tender leaves quickly and easily from their stems. He is methodical, though you catch him munching on a few. Meanwhile, brown the sausage and short ribs in batches in a large pot on the stove. See that he has finished and wants to do more. He is not usually so solicitous in the kitchen, so against your better judgment, tell him he can put some sausage into the pot.

Cringe as the oil splatters—just a drop—and burns him. Hear him scream and see him recoil from the kitchen, betrayed. Run his finger under cool water and comfort him. Explain to him that the kitchen can be a dangerous place, that injuries happen but most of the time we keep going. Tell him the story of your chef uncle cutting himself on that national cooking challenge show. How he kept cutting and ultimately won.

Understand that you are teaching him perseverance. Resilience. Resolve. Finish browning the meat and remove to a large bowl. Wipe his tears and tell him it's time to make the meatballs. Preheat oven to 350 and lightly oil a cookie sheet. Sure, you could fry them, but this will be easier, slightly healthier, less dangerous and just as good.

Wash your hands carefully and take off your wedding rings,

hand them to your son who stacks them on his thumb. Remember when this gold band that sits on top of your silver one belonged to your grandmother. Remember too that she never removed it to cook. How it was caked with meat and egg and breadcrumbs. Put all ingredients into the bowl. Put your hands into the bowl and mix thoroughly. It will be freezing, and your fingers will ache but you will keep going.

In your father's presence, you often felt small, silly, inferior, neglected.

In Dave's presence, you always feel capable, interesting, intelligent, appreciated.

Wash your hands again and get a little bowl of water, put it on the table between the bowl and the cookie sheet. Dip your hands in the water to keep the meat from sticking to them. Form small balls between your palms and place them onto the sheet. Tell your son the story of the woman you worked for who made meatballs by rolling unseasoned ground meat into balls and sticking them into the microwave. *How were they, mama? They were terrible, Rudy. Meat rocks, we called them. What did you tell her, mama? I told her they were delicious, Rudy.* See empathy and understanding flash across his face. Affirmed.

Bake for 15 minutes or so, turning once or twice.

In the same pot you browned the meat in, fry the onions, garlic, carrots, parsley and thyme in olive oil over medium heat. Cook until the onion is between translucent and slightly browned. Add tomato paste and cook until everything looks rusty. Add red wine to deglaze the pan. Cook down for a minute or two. Add canned tomatoes and water, the meat and meatballs back in. Salt and pepper to taste. Bring to a boil, then turn to very low, cover and simmer for 2-3 hours, stirring regularly so the bottom doesn't burn.

Forget your son's lesson when you lift the short ribs from the pot in two hours to test for doneness, and let them fall and splash back into the sauce, scalding your right hand so badly that tears unattached to Country Western music or memory come and your stomach turns over from pain. Suck your scream into your lungs to not terrify your children and stick your hand under cool running water. Keep it there. Ask your husband to stir the pot. Give yourself a few minutes—the pain will pass— and keep going.

Dave is just a year younger than your father was when he died. You are always hyperaware of this fact—at lunch at Wegmans, over beers at Zenos, at writing conferences, on play dates with the kids and here in the kitchen as you cook for him and his family. You wonder if he knows this. If he can sense it—an unspoken anxiety on the table between you. You find yourself looking at Dave, who looks nothing like your father, and your brain gets stuck. You always knew your father was young when he died—46 years old is young by anyone's standards. But here is Dave, your peer, your friend, a guy who grew up in the 80s like you, who writes about hair metal bands and still listens to Van Halen, loud. A guy. A word which is somehow closer to boy, you think, than man. But he's also a parent, a husband, a homeowner, a professional, a grownup. You can't make sense of this. You realize your father, too, was just a guy.

Your son is back and wants to dance with you and there is no better place to dance, you think, than the kitchen while Willie sings about blue eyes and rain at the end of the day. He looks up at you as and you remember the ICU nurses crooning over your father, his eyes they called "Paul Newman blue." The kitchen is filled with heat and light and delicious scent, your boy's own blue eyes now nothing but bright.

Willie and Waylon and Rudy and you dance close and twirl and dip while the ragu simmers. You'll serve it soon, sprinkled with cheese over Ziti, with bread and red wine from bottle and box. Note that these songs are duets, "musical compositions for two performers." You remember your father; you dance with your son; you cook for your friend.

❧ 3 ❧

TURTLE SOUP

It's the fall of my junior year of high school, and my father and I plan a trip to visit several colleges in eastern Pennsylvania. We have never, in my memory, spent so long a period of time together and I am both excited and terrified by the idea. My mother has engineered this, I suspect, as a way for he and I to "bond." Prior to this, our bonding consisted of him sitting in the crook of the blue loveseat in the family room, me sitting adjacent in the crook of the couch. End table and lamp between us, we make awkward, one-word comments as we watch Mutual of Omaha's *Wild Kingdom*: "Wow. Look. Tiger." "Yeah. Big. Teeth." What, I wonder, will we talk about on the 2½ hour car ride from our green and white Connecticut colonial home to the artsy, cobbled streets of Washington Crossing, Pennsylvania?

Mostly, I know, we won't talk. I will try to read but nausea from the car's motion will make the print wavy in front of my eyes and I will put *King Lear* or *Jude the Obscure* back in my bag. He will stare straight ahead at the road, steer with his right hand and flick the red tip of his cigarette out the cracked window to his left. The ash will blow behind us; the road will open up long in front and we will settle in.

"Grab me the tape in the glove compartment."

About an hour into the trip, my father points across the

seat, almost poking my chin in the gesture. I say nothing and pop the latch, reach in to retrieve what I'm sure will be Beethoven. Or opera. *God, not that.* I am pure pop these days: U2, Culture Club and Howard Jones. I have not yet learned to appreciate the richness of a Bach cello sonata or the layered intensity of a fugue.

I hand him the black cassette, its label a plain white sticker with red lines on which you are supposed to write in the name of the artist and the song title. But this one is blank. He turns it sideways and slides it into the slim rectangular opening and I hear the mechanism click on; the tape begins to move across the spools.

The air is suddenly filled with percussion and electric guitar and the car begins to jerk left and right. I don't know which phenomenon to focus on: the unlikely beat coming from the speakers, or the uncomfortable sensation as my shoulder blade bounces against my seatbelt. I decide on physical safety and turn to scan the lanes next to and behind us. There are no cars anywhere in our immediate vicinity. The music pounds to the rhythm of the bass, and the car continues its hurky dance:

Left, left, right, right... "a risin'... left, left, right, right, right...

I turn to look at my father for affirmation or explanation and see that he is still holding fast to his driving posture, eyes front and steely. But he has finished his cigarette and now both hands are on the wheel. He grins wildly but doesn't turn to look at me, doesn't say anything. I don't know how to talk about his driving, how to express my fear and my surprise that he would be reckless and playful in this way, so I turn up the music—*since when does he listen to Credence?*—and sing.

My father books us into the Washington Crossing Inn and makes dinner reservations before we even see our rooms. We are traveling around the coal region today, with appointments to meet with counselors at Lehigh and Villanova University. Part of me knows already that these will be futile visits—my grades are good, but not *exceptional.* My father, I'm guessing, knows this too. But still we pretend like this is a grand, important event.

"Remember to give the man a good strong handshake," he tells me. "No wimpy fish."

I cringe a little at this admonishment, because I sense his worry that I will come off like a *girl*. I am constantly aware that my father thinks I am wispy and afraid of my shadow; unadventurous and staid. I am only partially aware at seventeen that this goes beyond the particularity of *me*; that is also has something to do with women in general. The IBM executive doesn't know what to do with a soft-spoken, tentative *daughter*. I'm not like the women he works with—the power-suited, shoulder-padded managers who bark and wheedle deals. Or like the Australian businesswoman we hosted for Easter that year—making lewd jokes in our kitchen, her voice gravelly and rising above the others, my father's simply ringing with admiration.

The dining room is beautiful. Light from votive candles glances out through cut crystal holders making the whole place look warm and sort of golden. The linens are white and the room swirls with quiet and, what I imagine must be, meaningful conversation. We have been gone all day, and neither interview went well. Villanova wanted higher test scores and the man in the leather office at Lehigh might well have just laughed. Firm handshakes, it seemed, would not be my ticket into college.

He's been here before and knows what to order, so like at all of our fancy meals together, he chooses for me. I will always allow this, even as my feminist instincts begin to take root and flourish. Partly, it is because I feel overwhelmed by the details: the gold-rimmed plates, the silver butter dome, the lattice-backed dining chairs, and it is just easier to be taken care of. Partly, it is because I trust his taste; I know that he has been all over the world eating new, interesting food. I am thinking about my own upcoming adventure—college—and craving newness, surprise. I want to taste what he has tasted and know that I am not provincial, that I am worldly like him. I want him to know that I'm game.

Tonight, he chooses *Chateaubriand* for two tucked into buttery phyllo pastry and Caesar salad prepared table-side. He's showing off and we both know it. Speaking a little French (I understand), and a little Italian (I can guess at meanings), he sends the white-coated waiter, the harried busboy, all over the dining room and back to the bar several times. He wants a wine list, bottled water, a book of matches. He is not brusque with these people, nor is he particularly despotic. My father, when he chooses to be, is positively charming.

Just after the salad course with its rich, cloying dressing of yolk and mustard, the small, salty fish like punctuation marks on top, the waiter brings two white ceramic soup tureens, spoons and a crystal cruet filled with amber liquid. My father bends his head over the steaming broth and I can see and hear him inhale with pleasure.

"Turtle soup," he says. "Tremendous."

"Tremendous" has always been my father's hallmark word. It's the congregation of syllables he reserves for highest praise: delicious meals, beautiful classical compositions, high marks. In the fifth grade, when I brought home a spelling test with a grade of 97%, he asked me what happened to the other three points.

Turtle soup, though, is indeed tremendous. The broth clings to the back of my spoon and rich bits of smoky meat slip over my tongue like silk. My father takes several spoonfuls and then reaches for the sherry. He surprises me by pouring it first not into his bowl, but into mine.

"What was your favorite book in high school?" I ask him, dipping crusty bread into my bowl and feeling the first flush of the sherry settle on my cheeks. I have just finished a paper on two Ibsen plays, *Hedda Gabler* and *A Doll's House,* and I am feeling for the first time the intellectual excitement that comes with comprehension and synthesis. I have learned the power of the thesis statement—the way it organizes and collects, pulling all observation toward itself. I appreciate the way it governs a paper and helps the reader know what to expect.

"Oh, Shakespeare, Milton, I suppose. And Homer. The greats and their great characters. What else is there?"

He eats slowly: a sip of soup; a sip of wine. Thoughtful. His blue eyes large and pulsing behind wire-rimmed glasses. I think he looks and sounds like the most intelligent person on the planet and I am wholly enraptured; wholly intimidated.

My father, I know, majored in English and minored in philosophy in college. I also know that he started his studies at Iona College in New Rochelle, New York, right after high school, and finished them at Farleigh Dickinson University in Teaneck, New Jersey, a few years after I was born. What I do not know, and will not know for many years, is that my father never *really* finished his studies—never earned a degree of any kind. While at Iona, he worked days as a sanitation collector—a garbage man—and went to class in the late afternoon and evening. "Worked my way through," he had told me. "That and scholarship." He was the picture of industriousness and self-reliance. But this was only part of the picture.

The other parts—the frames he left out for good reason while talking to his college-bound daughter—were the ones that showed him and his best friend Dan on the Metro North train up to 125th street in Harlem on Thursday nights, in and out of bars and jazz clubs in the late 1960's. He left out afternoons spent on the banks of the briny Hudson River, shooting bb's at feral cats, a case of warm Budweiser cans in the trunk. They made it to work every morning but slept through or skipped their classes. My father grew up poor and Italian, Dan, poor and Irish. Neither of their families seemed to value education for education's sake, and in 1967, with the Vietnam conflict gaining momentum, that must have been what it felt like for them in the classrooms of a small Catholic college in suburban New York. So they dropped out and upped their drafts, both signing on for active duty in Saigon. Ironically, neither went. Dan ended up behind a desk in Germany, my father an MP in Anchorage, Alaska.

Turtle soup came into its heyday in England with the 1751 publication of *The Art of Cookery Made Plain and Easy* by Hannah Glass. Traditionally, marine turtles were used to make this thick, redolent stew. But it was not the turtle *meat* that gourmands prized. Turtle soup takes its texture instead from a rendering of the fat layer between the inner and outer shells. Apparently, the expense associated with the delicacy led to a somewhat short-lived food fashion, because by the 1800's, recipes for *Mock* Turtle Soup were appearing everywhere. Most of them call for a whole calf's head to be boiled down to that same gelatinous state and then seasoned with savory spices and an anointment of sherry. The result is a dish both exquisite and ingenious and, on the rarified palates of patrons like my father and me, there could scarcely be detected a culinary difference.

The fact that it has been illegal to eat the meat of marine turtles, in soup or otherwise, since the passing of the Endangered Species Act in 1973, is something my father could have learned during hours of tuning into his nature specials. He is a man loyal to the random fact, the odd tidbit. With him I learn that "nudibranch" is another way to say, "sea slug." I learn that you can eat the same seaweed we picked from the beach in Honolulu with a sesame oil dressing and that it will pop and crunch in your mouth like fish eggs. I also learn that enough sherry poured into your turtle soup from a crystal cruet held by your father, who is also drunk, will go straight to your head and give you the guts to keep asking questions.

"Why did you pick English?"

I ask him, mostly to hear him validate what I already know will also be my pick of majors. I have this image of us, father-and-daughter-scholars of the American Renaissance; the snooty-learned of our family, the first two generations of college graduates.

"It was the only door still open on deadline Friday."

My face, once a light flush, now burned with embarrassed realization: this man I had constructed so carefully as a focused intellect, and according to whose intellect I had so carefully constructed myself, had, at one time, been as lost and bungling as I had been on the ivied grounds of Villanova. Neither of us knew what we were doing and we were both in over our heads; surprised by how plans can go so far awry.

In the piano bar after dinner, my father gets that same glint he had in the car ride down from Connecticut, the one that says, "Watch me surprise you." He stumbles up to the microphone and says something to the piano player. He winks at me. I am seventeen and reeling with his insistence on all things edible, random and odd. The first notes of Nat King Cole's

"Nature Boy" plink out from the keys and my father begins to sing about a strange and enchanted boy who took a long trip.

This has been the strangest of meals; the most enchanted of trips. I believe there will be many more of them between us, so I work to cultivate and savor these delicacies; to keep the promise we make each other that night over salty small fish and glistening rich soup made with, or without, exotic reptile meat: *try everything at least once.*

4

SELF-PORTRAIT WITH
ROLLER COASTER

1. Action Park

See that chubby ten-year-old girl with the blonde ponytail at the bottom of the water slide? Watch her as she hauls that over-large black rubber donut back up the endless steps so she can do it again. And again. See her dowdy navy-blue swimsuit? After the third trip down the fake river, bouncing her butt against the gritty concrete bottom, it'll rip right along the worn seam in the back and she'll have to wrap a thin white towel around her waist for the rest of the day.

See her over there now, climbing up a different slope to the top of another water slide. This one's different: no chutes to funnel screaming park-goers into frigid bleached waters. They've covered the mountain with that same spongy stuff the mats are made of, and they're going to hose her down with a regular green garden hose. Will she sit or lie back? She can't be stupid enough to go down head-first, can she?

Oh dear.

See those bumps in the surface of the slide? They call those moguls and when she hits them she'll fly alright—ass over teakettle—all the way to the broken bottom where her father will be laughing his face off.

2. *Toronto's Wonderland*

They sit in the front car, always. The girl and her father, unlikely thrill-seekers, but only on roller coasters. In real life he hates chaos, won't drive into or around New York City. She still remembers the bike accident—scrape of metal, kiss of asphalt —and has never ridden again. But here they dare each other toward bravery and excess, climb into the front car of the double loop coaster at Toronto's Wonderland, feel the summer air push their hair around, their stomachs plummet with terror and elation, hear their synchronous screaming as they ascend and descend and ascend and descend.

3. *Six Flags Great Adventure*

It's going to storm. Gigantic grey clouds build on top of a blue-sky summer day and the rain begins softly enough. Maybe they can wait it out under the pavilion at the food court or in the gift shop at the front gates. Maybe it will pass and they'll still be able to go on the Flying Swings or the Tower of Terror. But there's no blow-over for park-goers today and six thousand people flock to the front gate, jam their bodies into metal turn-stiles that lead to the parking lot. It's raining, it's pouring. This is the kind of throng that tramples people at soccer games, rock concerts. Bodies jammed against metal. Hive mind and body. *Out! Out!* The girl and her mother hold hard to each other—a hub at the center of the chaos. *Where is your father? Why are the damn gates locked? Why are they locked!*

4. *The New Jersey Turnpike*

In the car on the way home, exhaustion emanates. Fatigue of the long, active day. Languorous. The girl and her sister sit in the back. They close their eyes and feel the thrum of highway as it climbs up through the tires. Their mother needs to stop to pee. *No*, he says. *Hold it*, he says. *Jesus Christ we just got on the road and I am not going to stop.* The girl feels her own empty bladder, imagines two or three Cokes filling it suddenly. Feels it stretch and scream. Her mother pleads. Her father flicks an ash from his cigarette out the window. The window is wide open. The girl and her sister open their eyes in time to see their mother's jewelry fly past their father, out and onto the ash-strewn road.

5. Lake Compounce

The girl lost her taste for roller coasters. Always sick on carousels and in back seats. Tender vestibular sense. See her sitting now with her niece on the Rocking Pirate Boat ride. Back and forth. Watch her watch the kid on the other side, hear his maniacal laughter, see him greening ominously. Back and forth. Back and forth. She clutches her niece hard to her body, prays they'll be on the upswing when the sick kid blows.

6. Rye Playland

Let's ride the Dragon Coaster, Daddy, and then walk the scrubby beach and get Italian ice. I like how its wooden skeleton groans as we go, want to feel it shake like a table with one short leg. Let's sit up front and pretend we are in that game, Mousetrap! Let's see who can do the best scream.

And then, in ten years, let's pretend you didn't tell me about the toddler ride, the tiny red airplane that loosed from the metal mechanism and truly flew.

7. King's Island

There are no lines today, so the girl and her mother ride the Tilt-a-Whirl as many times as they want. Get on, strap in, hold fast as the world tilts and whirls, neighboring rides a red and white blur. The summer air pushes their hair around, flicks the straw hats from their heads. Next, they enter the Rotor, a cylinder that spins them around and around and the floor drops out but they don't fall; instead the g-force splats them to the wall, sticks them there like insects, splayed and spinning 'til the bottom comes back up.

8. Park Forest Community Pool

The girl grew up and had kids. See her standing with her older one, every muscle of his body locked in inertia at the side of the water slide. His blue eyes wide, she can tell he wants to climb the endless steps and fling himself into the steep yellow tube. She knows the burn he'll feel in his thighs as he ascends to the platform, the flurry he'll get in his gut as he plummets. She knows the way the water will spray in his face, stopping his breath hard for just one instant before his lungs swell open again. She knows her son. She knows terror and body and danger and elation and welcomes them all to the slough at the bottom of the slide.

5

DEAD DAD DAY

It begins each year with a grocery list: green cocktail olives, a tub of cream cheese, Genoa salami sliced paper-thin, pepperoncini, Progresso-brand caponata (unless I have time to make it and I usually don't), bread sticks, hard Italian table cheese (maybe Fontina this year), Stone Wheat crackers, one piece of exotic fruit (star, kiwi, persimmon). Each year I prepare practically the same antipasto, give or take an ingredient depending on what I can remember. I chop the olives into the cream cheese and spread them liberally onto crisp crackers. I drizzle good balsamic vinegar over shards of pungent cheese. I wrap finger-slim breadsticks with prosciutto, salami, or sopressata—the marbling fat melting as it enters my mouth. I pop vinegar-tart green peppers one at a time and follow them with the strange and unlikely contrast of sweet fruit or savory eggplant.

Each year I also plan a dinner menu of something I have never made before. I look through my cookbooks for Italian, Spanish, Indian, or Korean dishes that look challenging and satisfying. I hold myself to the following criteria: the recipe must include more than three steps; it must be something new to me; I must be able to imagine sharing the meal with my father. When I find a recipe that meets all criteria, it is then time to invite my guests—usually only my two or three closest friends, those people who understand this ritual I've created to celebrate my father's life, and the name I've chosen for it: Dead Dad Day. The date is always the same: August 6, the last day of my father's too-short life.

This year I am rolling sushi with cucumbers, pickled radish, and shiitake mushrooms on my new bamboo mats. When I was a sophomore in college, my father took me to my first sushi bar in a little neighborhood of White Plains, New York. We had a habit of meeting for lunch then, as his office was just ten minutes from my campus. It was a surprising time in our relationship—me just beginning to live an adult life and him beginning a new one after his divorce from my mother. I always felt like we were on the edge of some new discovery about each other, and the weekly luncheons in local and ethnic restaurants only added to this sense of anticipation and mystery.

We walked into the cramped, dark space, ornamented with red paper fish banners and straw floor mats. I could tell he had been here before as he led me not to a table, but right to the bar where we could see the pink and grey fish glisten, the octopus and squid shine next to the chef's large knife. We sat on hard stools and my father ordered two cups of warmed sake for us while we deliberated our meal. The menu was entirely in Japanese, and though he often traveled to Tokyo for business, he didn't really know the language. Instead, he ordered based on the color photographs, pointing and nodding at the dour-looking sushi-chef for each selection. This was the day my face grew warm as rice wine, the day I learned about the sweet tang of miso soup, and the day I first tasted the soft, heavy salmon sushi I have come to love.

It's hard to remember what we talked about. More than likely, the conversation was about his traveling, his adventures in food and culture as an executive for IBM. Milk-fed New Zealand veal. Peanut satay on the street in Indonesia. Prawns, "this big," next to Sidney Harbor. I probably did a lot of listening; a lot of watching him gesticulate wildly as he bounced from talking about food to eating it, his wooden chopsticks moving with grace and punctuation among the sushi, the shumai, the edamame on the small counter in front of us.

Strangely, my father was not a talker unless he was either talking and eating or talking *about* eating. At least, he didn't talk much to me except for at these moments. Growing up, our family discussions were clipped and brusque. He worked sixty or seventy hours during the week and apparently did enough talking there. When he came home, he mostly sat on the couch, read the paper, and watched the Giants game, Charles Kuralt, or Nova. My father seemed to dwell in silence, and his silence swallowed all of us whole. My mother wasn't allowed to chitchat about her day at work (also at IBM—a way to get closer to him?) because that was "shop talk" and he wouldn't have it. My sister wasn't allowed to talk about her day at school because most of the time her presence irritated him out of wanting to hear her voice at all. Either she was wearing too much lipstick, or her skirt was too short. "Go upstairs and change," he would say. "Not another word."

I couldn't talk to him, though maybe out of all of us, I was the one allowed to. We might have talked about school because I was always doing well. I had learned to ask questions, to seek information neutrally, academically, and to defer to him for answers, so we might even have been able to talk politics and religion. We tried for a while, for as long as I had no real opinion of my own. But I was aware of the way he silenced my mother and my sister with his terse dismissals and, though I wanted nothing more than to garner his approval, to ally myself with him, I was mostly unable to use this meager allowance because I didn't want to hurt anyone. Later, conversations were all but impossible because of boyfriends he didn't like and my burgeoning liberal opinions about the world. But this was years later, and in the meantime, I learned to go without conversation and communicate with him instead through food.

Sunday mornings my father would leave before any of us were up, put on a pot of strong coffee, and head out to the market and the bakery. An hour later, he would stand at the butcher block kitchen counter pulling "gnoshy" foods out of the paper bag: hard and spreadable cheeses, stick pepperoni, Kalamata olives, crusty semolina bread. Sometimes he would also bring pastry: cherry turnovers, Lithuanian coffee cake, black and white meltaway cookies. This was his favorite way to eat, picking at small bites all afternoon, watching the Giants lose again. I would sit on the floor of the family room, next to the battleship hatch-cover coffee table he found at an antiques clearing house, and slice pieces of meat and cheese as he did. I felt close to him then. In communion.

My friends will be here in less than an hour, and I can't seem to get the sushi rolls to come out straight. Sticky rice is stuck to the counter, the cabinet doors, and the floor. The seaweed sheets won't stay together even after I moistened them with water. The truth is that I don't really know what I'm doing or how this will turn out, but I'm determined to get to the point where I will be dipping savory little packages into soy and wasabi, letting the burn wash my sinuses, wiping tears from my face as I reach for another and another. Part of Dead Dad Day, it seems, is a kind of gluttony. My father was a sensualist, a gourmand. I never saw him exercise any real restraint when it came to food or living. Not even after he was diagnosed with diabetes in his early forties. Even then we would find blue tins of Danish butter cookies under his bed. This was a man who entered a restaurant, knew the waiters' first names, and ordered one of everything.

My father died on August 6, 1992. He was 46 years old. He'd not been particularly well—he was insulin dependent and not monitoring his diet. He'd had a mild heart attack and developed pericarditis, an inflammation of the sac around the heart—but neither of these illnesses, as far as we can tell, contributed to his death.

   At first we thought he had suffered a stroke. He had woken up in his condo in Danbury, Connecticut one morning in late July to find that he could not walk. His left side muscles drooped. His speech was slurred and unintelligible. In the emergency room, he tried to talk to me, to yell, to continue a fight we had been having over my boyfriend at the time, but I couldn't understand anything he said. I could only see the frustration in his cramped hands, in his inflamed face. I remember I told him to calm down. That we could talk about this later. That he should concentrate on healing—there would be plenty of time to work this out.

That was the first day of his death. There would be nine more days that followed, but we didn't understand any of this right away. The diagnosis went quickly from stroke to bacterial infection of the brain, and the doctors began to treat him with a heavy regimen of strong antibiotics. He did not improve much, was still partially paralyzed, but seemed to get some of his speech back. He was moved out of ICU after two days and sent to a regular room. The expectation was that he would survive this infection, which had clearly damaged the area of the brain that governs motor coordination, and go on to a long rehabilitation.

During the days my father spent on the eighth floor, family from both sides overwhelmed the waiting room and the chairs next to his bed. My sister and my mother (now divorced from him) would flank his head, saying comforting, encouraging things, pouring him water from the sallow yellow pitcher and holding his head up while he sipped from the bendable straw.

Often, he would cry, which terrified me, as my father was not a man who expressed weakness or vulnerability. He was an academic, an intellectual. He analyzed and rationalized everything. I felt a small measure of comfort, my world-order reestablished, when the doctors explained that the crying was most likely a result of the way the infection had spread to the limbic system—the emotional center of the brain. He couldn't control it.

Most days I would sit in the straight-backed chair across the room and watch the people flit about him. I didn't know what to say to him, so I kept my distance. I felt like an outsider. I felt angry and sad as I watched my mother maneuver his pillows and adjust the bed angle. I watched my grandfather, his father, lather my father's face and then shave him, calling him "sonny boy" as he pulled the blade across in slow, careful swathes. This one image almost did me in entirely, and I still think of it as both the most loving and the most pitiful act I have ever witnessed. I watched my uncle, the restaurateur, feed my father a spoonful of his favorite pasta: farfalle with walnuts and peas in a tomato cream sauce. I knew this was a special treat for my father, as he had had very little solid food since being admitted. But he couldn't choke down more than a few small bites. A fungal infection had developed on his tongue and in his esophagus that made swallowing almost impossible.

When my father did not respond to the antibiotics the way the doctors had hoped, one young intern suggested that perhaps the infection was *viral*, not bacterial. His correct diagnosis came too late for the anti-viral drugs to really work, and one morning when I called the hospital to check on his condition, the nurse told me my father had slipped into a coma overnight. My family and I spent two more days in Danbury Hospital, waiting to see what would happen; waiting, really, for my father to die. By this time, we had a name for his affliction: viral encephalitis of unknown origin. He was pronounced brain-dead on August 4th, and on the night of August 5th, I went to his room, sat closer to him than I had been able to in the days before, and said goodbye. I knew I wouldn't be in there the next morning when the life-support machines were turned off.

I made the choice not to grieve publicly partly because the whole ordeal had been such a circus—family everywhere, crying, keening; disaffected doctors who couldn't say how or where he had contracted this disease; and the uncomfortable woman, the "Patient Liaison," assigned to our case. It was her job to prepare us for the hard questions: voluntary termination, autopsy, organ donation, funeral, cremation. I knew she was trying to help, but whenever I heard her rubber-soled shoes squeaking toward me and saw her face twisted into plastic pathos, I wanted to disappear. I knew my father would hate all of it too, so I opted out for both of us, crouching beneath the public payphone in the hallway, clutching a hot cup of tea, as my sister, mother, grandparents, cousins, uncles —even my boyfriend, at my request—all pushed inside my father's room, encircled his bed, witnessed, and filed out, weeping.

My sister and I came to the term Dead Dad Day together, a few years after our father's death. Though I cannot say precisely when, it must have been two or three years later because it takes that long to form a shell around grief, a mesh cage through which you can still feel, but which allows you to keep safe distance as well. We are our father's daughters, and he taught us to communicate through sarcasm and dark humor. I imagine that one year I called her, sensing that we should acknowledge the day but not being quite sure how to without descending into a funk. Even then I had an instinct to keep my real grief to myself. On the phone, we might have said things in our father's voice: "Y'okay?" and "Yep, me too." Terse and abrupt but underscored with concern. "Well," I might have said haltingly, nervously, "Happy Dead Dad Day." Did we laugh then? I don't remember. But today it's like a secret, sad joke between us.

Dead Dad Day is a phrase that depends on a particular kind of humor, and not everyone understands it. Our mother, I think, was initially shocked and undone by it, but now, with years, she too has come around to calling me and my sister on August 6 and wishing us "Happy Dead Dad Day—or whatever you call it." It's a phrase that perfectly reflects my complicated relationship to his death—my anger and my flippancy, on the one hand; my deep private grief that seeks company on the other.

When I cook elaborate meals for my friends on Dead Dad Day, it is akin to prayer. It is because I cannot remember my father without thinking about food, and it is because I cannot eat without remembering and missing him.

Today, in his honor, we will start with the antipasto, move on to the sushi (regardless of the state it's in), dip into cucumber salad with sesame oil and scallions, and sample steamed pork dumplings I bought at the Asian market across the street. We will not watch our portion sizes and will likely drink two bottles of Shiraz, toasting him many times. I want to swoon from food today. I want to be firmly in my body on the day my father's body failed. Because Dead Dad Day is for me as well. Choosing the recipe. Shopping for ingredients. Preparing the complex dishes on which we now dine—all while thinking of him and me and our trips to new flavors and textures. This is how I can talk to him about everything that has happened in my life since he's been gone. In his language. In ours.

❧ 6 ❧

BODIES OF SALTWATER

At fifteen I am still a virgin, though not by much, or by choice. I have fallen into what passes for love with an older boy—a senior who will leave for the Air Force right after graduation. In the months before he leaves, while school is winding up for the year, he woos me with an old-fashioned tenderness and respect that impresses my parents. They let him take me, in his mother's car, to a "sock hop social" at the VFW hall in nearby Putnam Lake, New York. I wear a grey wool skirt and a blue cardigan sweater so I will look truly "50's." I wear my blonde hair tucked demurely behind my ears. My mother offers me her pearls.

John chops cords of wood from the fallen trees on our property and uses the money—$200—my father pays him to buy me a sweet sapphire ring. It must seem to my parents that he is a throwback to their own dating era—the kind of boy who asks permission for dates, for handholding, for quick kisses on stoops beneath the amber wink of the porch light well before midnight.

In some ways, John *is* a gentleman: he refuses to sleep with me even though I am willing and even impatient to experience "real" sex. He says I am too young. I am, and eventually I will be grateful to him for his stubbornness, his unlikely 19-year-old wisdom. But even without going "all the way," we still manage to fumble deliciously with each other's bodies over and over again and everywhere we can manage: his basement, my back-yard, the slippery blue vinyl bench seat of his mother's 1980 Ford.

As summer approaches and he gets set to leave for basic training in Texas, my family makes our own preparations for the first and, as it will turn out, the only real vacation we will ever take together. Fifteen and hormonal beyond my parents' guess-ing, I kiss my steady love goodbye, feeling like the 1940's film starlet bidding farewell to her soldier boy off to war, and begin to anticipate fragrant pineapple groves and the impossible floral abundance of the Hawaiian Islands.

I cannot guess that I will eventually look back on this trip and see it as the apex—the moment just before everything unravels and we finally fray into separate strands of the same threadbare blanket. Before Hawaii, I know as little about my parents' appetites for each other as they know of my ever-advancing expeditions into the territory of my own body. This summer, each of us, my parents, my younger sister, and I will give ourselves bodily to the heady breeze, to the slow stroke of the ocean, because each of us is suffering from some kind of willingness and impatience and needs to be touched by something.

The morning of our flight, everything is already out of sync. My mother and sister and I were up late last night doing wash and laying out our clothes in neat rectangles on our beds. My father worked late, finishing up his projects before vacation. He won this trip for us, or, more accurately, he *earned* it by designing an internal mail system at work. The award came with a $10,000 bonus which he put toward our trip. We will travel in style: first class seats for all of us, and the nicest accommodations in both San Francisco, where we will be stop-ping for two short days, and then Oahu and Maui, where we will lay in the sun, smelling the jasmine-air, for the better part of two weeks.

We wake the morning of our trip to the phone screaming at 7AM: my grandmother calling to wish us safe travels. We, all of us, scramble frantically at the sound. Our plane out of New York leaves at 9AM and LaGuardia is an hour and fifteen-minute drive from our home in New Fairfield, Connecticut, not to mention we need time to park the car and check in. We overslept by two full hours.

"Let's go, let's go, let's GO!" My father's voice punctures my sleep-logged brain like a drill bit. "No time. Grab your stuff. Let's go!"

The house is a whirlwind. Throw clothes on. Stick tooth-brush in mouth. Pull fingers through hair. Gulp breakfast—orange juice—straight from carton. Jump in car. Drive like mad. Curse. Curse. Park. Open trunk... *we just might make it...*

In the parking lot, the open mouth of the trunk spews forth my parents' suitcases and my mother's garment bag onto the asphalt. My sister and I stand there, staring, agape. *Empty. Where were our bags? Where were our clothes? Empty.*

But we have no time to wonder because now it is time to sprint for the gate. And this we do, just like in movies, together, a flock of family winging as fast as they can to catch their flight to paradise. We make it, with, it turns out, a little time to spare. Enough time for my sister and me to complain, dumbstruck, "Where are our bags?" Even as I say this, as soon as the ques-tion forms in my mind, I see them: two smallish suitcases packed with brand new shorts, halter tops and swimsuits, sitting next to the door like happy puppies waiting to be walked.

"I thought you guys had them," I whine to my mother. Now what would we do? I literally have the clothes on my back, travel clothes—jeans and an embarrassing red sweatshirt adorned with a polar bear, hardly the gauzy ensemble appro-priate for tropical climes—and one sundress tucked into the garment bag. No underwear. No swimsuit. My sister has even less.

"You girls are old enough to be responsible for your own things." My father's admonishment corrals us into the boarding line, and I wait to be told, *That's just tough. You'll have to make do.* Instead, unexpectedly, he laughs. He laughs all the way through the line and onto the plane and into his seat. He laughs when we step off the plane ten hours later, into the hot Hawaiian wind. My father started laughing in the airport and doesn't stop —not even while we shop in the expensive tourist stores on Waikiki for new clothes, hundreds of dollars' worth of floral shirts, bikinis and plastic flip-flops for each of us. He laughs and laughs. In my memory, he laughs for two whole weeks.

The image of my father laughing in the airport upon discovering our mishap has stayed with me throughout my life since then. In my mind, it shares company with only a handful of other moments wherein some other part of him—I want to think, some vital part of him—bubbled up from somewhere unknown to me, to my sister and likely even our mother. Laughing instead of scolding in the airport. Playing rock music instead of opera in the car. Clutching my hand hard and crying from his hospital bed.

I think of these moments as scenes because, truly, they felt cinematic, scripted. The stuff of fantasy. Were I writing the story of my life as fiction, these would be the "out of character" moments, the ones no reader would trust or believe.

Outside the Honolulu International Airport in the shocking sunlight, I stare, incredulous, at the massive, craggy mountain growing up and up and up from the volcanic Hawaiian earth, into and above the clouds, larger than, taller than, and altogether beyond my comprehension. The next time I'll be this close to a real mountain—not the soft green peaks of New York and Connecticut's Berkshires—will be near twenty years later, flying over Mt. Rainer in the Cascades. I'll have a similar reaction then—the feeling of being disoriented and displaced by more than just geography. A sense of being someplace utterly new.

Waikiki hums like one of the garish neon signs summoning tourists from the windows of countless trinket stores on the strip—the whole city a tacky-bright advertisement for itself. We arrive in Honolulu during the day, but my most vivid memories will be of the bustle of nighttime. Stores open until midnight or even all night. People milling through and about, adults and children, the steady chatter of commerce all around. Walk down to the beach and find Bible salesmen always awake, always proclaiming the Good News, unexhausted. Down a little further, bodies entwined and glowing under a postcard moon. The wakeful, continuous surf.

I am all too aware of my own body on the beach in Waikiki. The inheritor of my mother's pale Irish skin, I am used to dousing myself with sunscreen in the summertime. In the fourth grade, at the class pool party at Kevin McCarthy's house, our teacher, Sister Agnes, had ruined any chance I might have had of impressing the boys (Kevin, in particular) with my lovely brown (brown?!) one-piece when she took one look at my blue-white complexion, and announced, "You'll burn to a crisp, child!" I was shocked but mute as she wrapped me from head to toe in beach towels, slopped zinc oxide across my nose and plunked me, all but mummified, onto a lounge chair. I never made it into the pool.

Even slathered in SPF 30, I still manage to burn in weirdly shaped patches in Hawaii, and for a few days I glow as brightly as those neon signs on the strip by the beach. Neon signs, neon skin and the ubiquitous neon fashion of the 1980s—for a girl who spent most of her time demurring to others and trying to fade into the background, I must be quite the vibrant sight.

Besides the polar bear sweatshirt and jeans, I wore on the plane, the only other piece of clothing that made it with me all the way from home is my orange sundress. It is brighter than pumpkin, but not obnoxiously so, with graphic swirls and shapes in blues and greens and yellows. Princess cut with a sweetheart neckline and straps wide enough to hide evidence of my not-optional bra, it creates astonishing cleavage and I love it.

My father, who has no history of complimenting or even commenting neutrally on my mostly conservative clothing choices, but who is infamous for his harsh and chastising critiques of my sister's much racier wardrobe items (skintight acid-wash jeans, white fringe leather jacket), is either too preoc-cupied by the ocean and the palm trees to notice his eldest daughter's womanly figure on display, or he has chosen to ignore it.

We spend a week on Waikiki and do things tourists do. We swim and sun ourselves and shop for necklaces strung with sun-washed shell and coral. My sister and I stuff ourselves with the sweetest pineapple I have ever eaten and drink sparkly water with lemon or virgin versions of the tropical concoctions to which my parents add rum. We take catamaran tours, and I hang my head over the side of the boat, queasy from the choppy waves, and let the continual spray hit my face. In a picture taken by the tour captain—one of those "candid" shots they charge you extra for—my father sits between my mother and me. My knees are tucked up under my chin and I'm wearing an expression that might be sick or sleepy or just plain relaxed. "Hawaii, 1986" scrolls across the bottom of the photo in red cursive script, marking the exact moment in time for me, as if I could ever forget it.

La Mer at the Halekulani Hotel holds the honor of being Hawaii's longest, consecutively ranked AAA Five Diamond Restaurant, but all I know about it is that my father has, as per his usual, sought out the most opulent restaurant on the island and booked us a reservation before we'd even arrived. Maybe the original reservation was made for a table of four, but when we sit down at the white-clothed table lit with candles and moonlight, there are only three. Absent from the sailing picture, absent from dinner, my sister is off somewhere on her own. I understand how strange this is, how unquestionably unconventional. She is only thirteen years old and my parents have allowed her ridiculous freedoms on this vacation. She is adorable and brave; friendly to everyone and enormously spir-ited. She is not only *not* shy, she is what my grandmother, my mother's mother, might call "brazen."

Later tonight, as I walk back to our hotel ahead of my parents on the beach, I will come across her lying in sand just off the path, entwined with a boy whose orange hair glows as bright as my orange sundress. I will try to warn her, but it will be too late. Our father will summon her with us, back to the room. He will sit her down on the bed and lecture her for five minutes before allowing her to go back out "with her friends." I will wonder then if I am in some kind of bizarro world where my sister's "disobedience" and "bad behavior"—the same kind that usually get her grounded, screamed at, threatened and demeaned at home; the kind that will dovetail with her downing a bunch of over-the-counter pain pills in a few years; that will land her in residential drug treatment centers, and, eventually, when my parents feel like they have no other way to help her, to "save" her, a behavior modification facility-cum-high school for at-risk youth in the remote wilderness of northern Idaho—is being re-imagined as simple teenage spirit. Or celebrated. Or ignored.

Tonight, despite my sense of unease, I don't question her absence, probably because I am thrilled to have my parents' attention all to myself. Beyond the normal sibling tensions between us, the added element of "Good Daughter" vs. "Bad Daughter," makes me crave parental affirmation even more greedily than usual. I like the feeling, however false, however unfair, that I am being rewarded for my upstanding moral character. My parents don't really know me, yet.

The ocean breaks so close to the table that we can feel the spray while we eat. The moon takes up the whole black sky. I wrap the heavy-sweet smell of Plumeria flowers like a shawl around my bare shoulders, and eat, as I always do, whatever my father orders for me. The meal is the very definition of leisurely, taking something like four hours to enjoy, and punctuated with grunts of approval and sighs of ecstasy emitting from both my parents and from me. We eat lavishly, but the only thing that will stay with me is the seaweed appetizer that comes at the very beginning. Not like the seaweed salad I will come to love in sushi restaurants with my father during college —crunchy, vegetal strips of bright green flecked with red pepper flakes and slicked with sesame oil. This is something just as delicate but more pungent, tasting of ocean and sun, mineral and night, the green-black filaments swell into tiny orbs inside our mouths. We roll them on our tongues before popping them, like fish eggs, salty, against our teeth. Whimsical. Sensual. Delicious.

When dinner is over, my father suggests we walk back to our hotel along the beach. I walk behind my parents with my sandals in my hand. The night air is still warm, the white sand moonlit and cool against my feet. Despite this beauty, I feel my mind jump to worry about the upcoming school year to college and beyond. Junior year, I have been warned, will be the most difficult academically. I have seen the juniors carrying stacks of textbooks so high that their faces are hidden, only a tuft of hair or maybe eyes bleary from too much studying visible as they shuffle the halls between classes. I am already a worrier, and school is my job—my parents have always made this clear. They have expectations about my performance, my ability. I am a good student, even a *very* good student, but acutely aware that I am still not in the top 5% of my class. I am not the cream on top. Where will I get in? What will I do with my life?

I distract myself from my worry by settling back into my body. I think about John, who I will break up with when we return, and his sure hands and soft lips, our furtive make-out sessions under stairwells between classes. The only time I have ever been reprimanded by a principal was this spring with John. *Squillante, I swear if I come around one more corner to find you lip-locked with that boy....* I was horrified by the public chastisement —*I'm a good girl!*—but it didn't stop me. I just got smarter about where and when and for whom I unbuttoned my blouse.

My parents keep up their unhurried pace fifteen feet or so ahead of me as we make our way down the beach. My mother wears gauzy white pants and a loose tank top through which I can clearly see her bra strap and the outline of her underwear. My father wears a look that will always define him in my memory, even long after he is gone: khaki shorts and a neat polo shirt, brown leather deck shoes without socks. I can see the deep, mouth-shaped gouge on his thin, wiry calf from where the dog mauled him as a child. I watch his muscles twitch and flex with motion. They walk in what seems to be their usual disconnected silence, and then, quite suddenly, they stop.

I slow and watch as they turn to face each other, grinning wildly, emitting an energy I have never felt from them before. They haven't said a word to each other that I can hear, but my father takes his wallet out of his pants pocket. My mother removes her earrings. He takes off his glasses. She kicks off her shoes. I catch up.

"Here, Sheil," my father says. "Hold these for a minute." They hand me their various adornments and then take each other's hand.

There is one picture, from my first year of life or maybe the year before, of my father sitting in an easy chair, and my mother, in her plaid bell-bottom slacks, sitting in his lap. He has, in that classic tender gesture, placed a hand on each of her cheeks and has drawn his lips into an exaggerated pucker. I always loved this picture. It looked like love and laughter all at once.

But I have never before in my actual life seen the open, obvious affection or attraction they are showing each other and me until this night in Hawaii. Do they love each other? It looks like it, but I don't trust this. I don't really know. Nor do any of us know that their time is almost up. That there will be only four more years of marriage and increasing tension, bitterness and betrayal between them, or that my father's very life will be over in just six. None of that knowledge is available to us on the beach after our extravagant meal and *thank goodness*. There is only right now, these versions of us with our happily filled stomachs, our bodies lying in dune grasses or moving through salt air and strangeness, all of which we embrace.

My relationship with my father has always been constrained by his buttoned-up reserve, or maybe just discomfort with his own unwieldy emotions. My mother tells me regularly "He's just not demonstrative, Sheila, but you know he loves you." Eventually, he will demonstrate. He will weep uncontrollably from his hospital bed before he slips into a coma and dies. He will clutch hard at my hand and say all the things daughters hope to hear from fathers. But until then, his stock reply to the proclamation, "I love you, Dad," will always be a stingy and guarded, "Me too." I have accepted it as the best he can do.

So, imagine my surprise, my shock and utter delight, as I hold on to their stuff and watch my parents walk hand-in-hand, fully clothed, happy (oh I hope they are happy) and unguarded, into the rising white applause of a dark Pacific surf.

BODY OF WORK

I.

I have never seen myself naked.

This is not a metaphor; I mean that I have truly never in my life really looked carefully at, pondered or appreciated my body —my actual, physical form—in its own skin and nothing more. I never stood in front of a mirror as a teenager, monitoring my developing curves, nor as a grown woman, assessing changes to the landscape after childbirth. While I have a general sense of the shape of things—I have caught glimpses, accidentally—I have no clear knowledge of what I would see if I *really* looked.

Sunday was my 40th birthday and I have been writing *this* piece in other essays, poems, and in my head since I was at least 13 years old. In my diary that year, the one with the blue gingham cover pocked with pen marks and scratches, puffy hearts drawn all over the inside pages, there are only three entries, written over and over again: I Love a Boy Who Thinks I'm Stupid; Something Bad is Going on With My Parents; I Am So Disgusting That I Can't Even Look at Myself. It's become part of my identity: "the girl who has never beheld her own naked shape," in one poem; the one who cannot "imagine the unseen surface" of her own back in another. In each, a tone of disapproval, admonishment, an unspoken *knock-it-off-already-you-know-better.*

Though I announce my ignorance with what might seem like confidence and naked (ha.) bravery, I am not proud of this. In fact, as a woman, a mother, a feminist, and, it turns out, a writer, it is one of my greatest shames.

It's probably obvious why a poor body image would be concerning for the first three of those selves, and I could offer far too many theories (most predictable) about how I ended up so impressively wacked out about this. But what interests me at the moment is a strong sense that my corporal alienation is also tied inextricably to my writing self. It's a nagging kind of sensation, and one I've long wanted to work out on the page, shifting the pieces around to see how they might connect, what they might offer up.

2.

Peter wants to kiss me. He mumbles this sort of in my direction, eyes anywhere but on my face. I am twelve years old, and in my memory, we are sitting, for some reason, on the floor of my parents' bedroom, our backs nervous—stiff and aching against the bed. I have never been kissed before, though many of the girls in my seventh-grade class are already playing Two Minutes in the Closet with boys at parties to which I am not invited. I can see Peter in my periphery, turning his head and leaning in. I keep my back straight and turn my head too; it doesn't occur to me yet to move my whole body toward a kiss. I don't remember the kiss beyond that moment of decision and approach; have no memory of skin or lips or tongue. What I remember—what I will transcribe into countless diary entries, free-writes and onto the blank page of my self for years to come—is what he said after: "You know, you are really beautiful from the waist up."

3.

I live in my own periphery, my full-length reflection a thin sliver of only one side of me. My approach to mirrors, windows, the shine off of cars in the parking lot, purposefully avoidant, my image askew. Head, hair, face, eyes, shoulders, sometimes breasts, those are easier, acceptable even to me. Those I can look at. Otherwise, I either view myself in sections, incoherent parts of a whole, or not at all.

4.

Open on my desktop at this moment are two files, each containing a full-length manuscript of poetry—*my* poetry. I have been tending, polishing, readying them for the endless contest circuit. I have read them each countless times, and I quite like them both. I think there are readers who will respond to them, should I be lucky enough to get published. These manuscripts could not be more aesthetically different from one another. One is firmly narrative, largely autobiographical, shot through with longing and nostalgia and loss. The other is more deeply rooted in language and the beautiful and perplexing shapes it can make. It is fragmentary, associative, a little surreal. I joke that in the unlikely event that these books showed up next to each other on a reader's shelf, that reader would be very confused indeed about who the writer is.

Though I have long espoused a philosophy of *both/and,* rather than *either/or* in poetry—I read work from both traditions, have obviously written in both, and hear my voice naturally in both—the idea of claiming them both publicly makes me more than a little anxious.

5.

After my divorce, I enroll in a writing workshop at my local university. There, I enter into a dalliance with a fellow writer. He is, like most of the other men in my life to this point, confident, assured, opinionated and searingly intelligent. For months he keeps me at arm's length physically. The night we finally fall into bed, our pillow talk turns to poems. To my poems—the ones about my father's death—which he has read and about which he has readied the following commentary: "You know, no one really wants your emotional baggage." I don't remember responding; I don't think I could have. I remember putting my clothes back on quickly and then driving him home.

. . .

6.

A poem should look
Poems should face each other
Poems should echo
Poems should or shouldn't be poking you in your eye
A poem should sit a while
A poem should ride on its own
A poem should be different from your expectations
A poem should be on the moon
A poem should always have birds in it
Poems should radiate lots of affection
Poems should do without any comment
Poems should be in plain text
Poems should include a baby girl
Poems should be *I'm in love, damn it!*
Poems should progress
Poems should be read aloud to children
Poems should be lingered over
Poems should move
Poems should not be relied upon too heavily

7.

My lover and I kneel facing each other on the floor of my college dorm room, running our hands frantically over exposed flesh. I am so caught up in his body, in mine, that I have forgotten the full-length mirror hanging on the inside of the door. I turn my head to allow him better access to my neck and accidentally see myself—the curves of my breasts and hips, thighs, knees, slope of calves, feet. I make myself look for a long, shocked moment and think, is that really what I look like? Is that woman really me?

8.

If I publish manuscript #1, some of the confident, assured, opinionated men in my life will continue to pat me on the head and send me on my quaint, confessional way. They will not want my "baggage." If I publish manuscript #2, some of the others will roll their writerly eyes and use words like "pedantic" and "pretentious." They will wonder where I went, why I have eschewed the world of the body. When I worry over this, one man—a friend and himself a poet—will ask (again), "Why do you care so much about the opinions of men who really don't matter?"

9.

[insert death of confident, assured, etc. father here]

10.

My favorite poems are simple and direct, glittery gems hand-hewn from mineral rock, grounded in the sensual world, in human relationships. I roll them between my teeth and tongue.

My favorite poems are painterly abstractions, elliptical gestures, unfinished thought. They invite me in and then inflate with impossible language, float above me, just at the limit of my reach.

11.

I am nine months pregnant with my first child, my son. I step out of a hot shower, hotter than I'm supposed to take, and reach for a towel. As always, I stare straight ahead at the towel bar opposite the tub, perpendicular to the sink and the mirror. But something moves in the corner of my eye, and before I realize, before I remember not to look, I have turned to follow it. Through the humidity and behind the scrim of steam I see my belly, breasts, hips, mouth. Eyes filled with relief and bright wonder.

12.

My naked body is pretty much like any other naked body
My naked body is a humiliating example
My naked body is unlikely, thrilling

My naked body is sensual in the extreme
My naked body is not what it was in pre-baby days
My naked body is an affront
My naked body is a participant
My naked body is these potato chips
My naked body is now hidden under the table
My naked body is as beautiful as my naked thoughts
My naked body is the least of your concerns
My naked body is the blank page

13.

Here is what I want:

I want to look directly into the mirror and learn my shape, begin to know it first without judgment, then with appreciation. With praise.

I want to spend this decade unafraid and unashamed.

I want to knock it off, already.

I want to throw out the Book of Poetic Shoulds. Open my arms wide.

I want to walk into my 40s full-ready to embrace every line, every lump, every word:

I lived it. I made it. I claim it.

MIX TAPE FOR A TOO-YOUNG MARRIAGE

1994
Alternative Songs
#4—The Cranberries, "Linger"

I took your name, slipped into it like the thousand dollar dress made from Italian lace I could not afford. Egg-shell blue on the church walls and the trees not quite rusting outside. We timed it poorly, for pictures, we said. Even now, even these many years later, when I tell the story about the forkful of cake and frosting, the ritual impact at the back of my throat, the choking while smiling for photos, the blood, the infection that followed, I say, and mostly believe, it was only a champagne miscalculation. So, cheers to us, new husband. I was tipsy, too. I pretended not to see you.

1995
Adult Contemporary
#6—Sheryl Crow, "Strong Enough"

Why don't you write more? You should take writing classes. You should find your own friends. I'm not staying at this restaurant. It's not well-lit. I don't care if we already ordered—I'm leaving. You figure it out. We don't have enough misery in our life. You should get a job in a call center. You should go to jewelers' school. I'm going out after work. Your grief is exhausting. You don't really miss your father. He was an asshole. So what? Another half-assed award for a half-assed writer. Why don't you write more about me? You don't understand. She's a good friend. She's going through a hard time. I feel like I need to be there for her. She's my angel. Don't stay up. I don't know when I'll be home.

1996
Hot Modern Rock Tracks
#5—The Counting Crows, "Long December"

New Year's Eve at the Hilton. Color-enhanced salmon fillet. Twice-baked potato. Stale roll. Butter rosettes in a bowl full of ice. Pasty green beans with sliced almonds, charred and bitter over top. $150 per head, please, for this sad plate, sad date. A week ago at Christmas, there had been family, shiny ornaments and a promise, *for next year*. A feeling of tentative optimism. There had been the earlier assurance, *she's just a good friend*. But tonight, there is a terrible wedding band playing someone else's favorites and a pair of too tall heels. There is a fever—an actual fever—and a table where she is part of a pattern: wife, husband, wife, husband. There are whispers and shoulders that dip and brush, bodies turning not very subtly toward each other. There is so much to drink. It's going to be a long night. She wishes this were a fever dream. Why are they here? Why did he arrange this? Why did she believe him at all?

1997
Radio Songs
#1—Shawn Colvin, "Sunny Came Home"

I'll meet you at TGI Friday's or someplace well-lit. I could go for some wings. Bring the paperwork and I'll sign it. I'm not going to court with you because I don't have to. That's the law. I'll keep you on my health insurance until you get a real job (why don't you work in that jewelry store?) because I'm kind. I don't understand why we have to get divorced at all. I see this as just one point on the continuum of our relationship. Yes, I live with her, but we're more like roommates at this point than anything. It says on page six that you want your name back. Why? Why do you sound so mad? I'd be honored if you kept my name.

1998
Billboard 200
#2—Madonna, "Ray of Light"

I peeled away the August heat, stripped off responsible brown silk, set paperwork down on the dining room table. Cool glass top, calm blue bottles on a white windowsill in my best friend's apartment. She stood with me while the judge, come out from chambers, wagged his finger at my youth, my lack of respect for "the institution." Wag, wag. She shuffled the papers back into order. She filed them for me with the bailiff. And where is your husband? Why isn't he here with you? How do I know he knows you're here? Young lady. Young lady, you'll have to revise this paragraph. The one that wants your name back. I don't like it. Revise it because I can make you. It's the law. Again. $35. Re-file. Pay up. One year and six months. My friend and I sat in windows and watched the breeze bump lace. We drew smiles and initials into heads of beer and licked ambivalence from our fingers. I slept with women and men and re-learned my pleasure. She was a good friend. I was going through a hard time. She was there for me. She loaned me postage. We whirled to music on her wooden floors in August heat, light shooting from our fingertips. Again. Again. I revised my way back to my old name, into my new life. I paid for everything.

❧ 9 ❧

VESTIARY

1979

Our dryer's broken and my fourth-grade blue plaid Catholic school uniform crackles with static and sticks to my pilling sweater tights. My mother teaches me to sprinkle water on my skirt to break the charge. I do this in the bathroom after lunch and Diane, a popular girl, sees. For the next three years I cry as my classmates taunt me, call me, among other things, "static cling."

1980

My teacher tells me all girls have to wear white blouses and red or green skirts for the Christmas pageant. My mother tells me I *must* wear a bra, I absolutely need one. I am the only girl in my class who does, and I make her promise, make her *swear to me that you can't see its outline through the white cotton*. During "Silent Night," we have to stand on stage with our back to the audience and I can feel a room full of eyes and her lie.

1982

On rainy days I wear my favorite dress to school. It's a confection of vivid blue, yellow and red sateen with a drop waist and, looking back, quite clownish. But I still believe in ruffles and flounce. Believe I can will a grey sky bright.

1983

Peter and I sit on the shag rug of my bedroom. We are listening to Asia or Air Supply or Styx. He turns to kiss me. It will be my first and we've known each other since we were babies in cribs. My light blue chinos strain against my hips and my already-developed breasts heave (*please!*) fetchingly. I close my eyes because I am supposed to and he says, "You know, you are really beautiful from the waist up."

1985

I am in Hawaii on our family vacation. Patchwork of pale and sunburned skin. My orange sundress glows bright as the neon signs on the strip in Waikiki. My boyfriend is leaving for the air force in August and will not sleep with me because he thinks I am too young. I am. My orange sundress has a plunging sweet-heart neckline that creates astonishing cleavage and I love it.

1988

My father and I pose for pictures in the living room before my senior prom. Hot pink strapless satin and big blonde hair because nobody had any taste in the 80s. Crystal baubles borrowed from my best friend who will sing "Ave Maria" at his funeral in a few more years.

1992

My father died in the hospital three hours ago and now I'm at the Casual Corner in the Danbury Fair Mall, shopping for his funeral. I have tried on five or six black dresses and nothing fits. My body resists every fabric, every neckline, every hem. Some-how, the nurse who cared for him is here. She was off this

morning, so she doesn't know. She approaches me, smiling. I
crumple and she catches me. My best friend tells me it's okay to
wear separates, so I buy a black linen blazer and a skirt bright-
ened by frantic yellow sunflowers.

1994

I stand in front of a wall of mirrors at the bridal shop. I puff
and billow, a silly white cloud. A ringing bell. My grandmother,
who was not invited to this fitting, gasps to my mother, "Oh!
She will look just beautiful in that once she loses all that
weight."

1998

I have been sitting in the Meriden Courthouse since 8am. I am
not on the docket and my husband's not here, because, even
though he's the one living with his girlfriend and asked for this
divorce, *fuck the system, man.* My stack of meticulous forms sits
in the hands of the bailiff. My brown silk suit, bought to
impress and prove myself stable, responsible, darkens with
sweat and sticks to me in the stale air. It's 4PM when the judge
calls me forward to say *young people take marriage too lightly* and
how old are you, young lady? and *no, I won't grant your divorce today,*
and *where is your husband, anyway?*

2002

It's my first date with the man I will eventually marry, the one
who will become my life partner, the father of my children.
Love of my life. I don't think twice about what to wear. My new
uniform: soft red V-neck sweater that clings lusciously like he
will to my astonishing curves, A-line denim skirt, and tall black
boots that I will need to teeter in on tiptoe to hug him hello.

2011

My black, knee-high Doc Marten boots—the ones I lusted after but was nowhere near punk rock enough for in 1987—arrive in the mail. I am 41 years old and the mother of two but fuck it. I lace them all the way up and dance around the house to The Clash.

2012

A student, a young woman, pulls me aside in the hallway outside of my office. *I'm sorry*, she whispers, hesitant, blushing, *but your skirt is up in the back.* I laugh, thank her, then reach behind me, pull it out of my tights. Static sparkles in the air between us and all around.

10

FOUR MENUS

I.

We're eating Korean soup tonight. *Yook gae jang*—shredded beef with cellophane noodles, scallions, and some long, fibrous mysterious vegetable. And spice—mouthfuls of red oil that make my nose run and my tongue sing. I am in love with the man across the table whose nose is running too. We glisten and are happy. Happiness is the long tails of soybeans slicked with sesame oil, the strings hanging from our mouths. We sip soup and poke at condiments with our wooden chopsticks—the kind that snap and splinter but who cares? I skewer a piece of jellied fishcake; bring it quivering to his lips. Another new, unexpected texture. When we eat together for the first time, it is before knowledge. Before the waitress knows our spice preferences: his flaming, mine not meek but milder. Before she has suggested other menu items (*Dol sot bimbim bab* crisping in hot Korean crockware) and even steered us clear of some (codfish soup—bland, no depth, not good). All before we know where our tastes will take us. I am a self-proclaimed gourmand, have tried everything offered to me at least once, but I have never before this first night eaten the Korean pickled cabbage called kimchi. I know nothing of the way its slight carbonation will incite, the way its crunch will satisfy. It's a revelation, that first bite. I feel extended; I surpass myself. The whole room ferments! Poetry! Kimchi! Philosophy! Later, when we sit kissing on my second-hand couch, he will exclaim, "I love your eyebrows!" and I will touch them and fall.

2.

Food is love. Samuel Butler said, "Eating is touch carried to the bitter end." I understand. I was in Paris with friends. We sat in a park where parents played with their children, bundled in colorful wools for the early March chill. They kicked yellow balls, ran laughing after each other, their hoods flapping behind them. "I want to eat them!" I exclaimed. I am 32 years old and childless. I am childless and in love with a man who's not sure he wants children. Some days I crave. I am a lean witch cackling hungrily into a bone-cold wind.

3.

In my twenties, I was voted "Most Succulent" among my closest friends. We had just seen a film in which plane crash survivors must resort to cannibalism among the wreckage and the snow. After, it was decided that my ample figure paired with my high energy would make for the tastiest meat. We made a pact: "If we ever crash on top of a snow-topped mountain and I die, you have my blessing to eat me." *Blessing*: an invocation of good fortune. If we crash and I die, I hope they are blessed with the warmth of a fire and time for slow cooking, for dining with relish and reverence, knowing that my spirit hovers, toasting their survival.

4.

For some, food is an inconvenience, something that wastes time. No. Food *extends* time, slows it for us generously. I cook because I believe in a slow life, a life of praise. I cook for my friends because I see them as divine. I cook to make holy moments, to call out and to reflect. I cook complex recipes in atonement. I gave up religion long ago. Now Sundays are for another kind of supper—one that acknowledges the sacrifices of human relationships. Sundays are for mundane tomato sauce stirred through with thyme and oregano and worship for the sensual world. It's a kind of worship that makes it impossible to ignore the implication of the body, the way food changes us, fills us with our own good, hearty love. Food is worship and God, to me, is kimchi, Kalamata olives, artichoke hearts, and roasted garlic popped hot from its skin and spread warm with butter on bakery bread. God is lamb shanks braised long in orange juice and Cabernet; is chopping Spanish onions with a heavy knife; is bittersweet chocolate chunked from dark Swiss bars. Is bittersweet entirely.

11

ROCKY'S MANICOTTI

Serves four people and three ghosts

For the Batter
6 eggs
Pinch salt
6 heaping tbsp flour
1 ½ cup milk

For the Filling
1 lb ricotta cheese
½ lb mozzarella cheese, shredded
1/4 cup fresh parsley or 1 tsp dried
3 or 4 eggs
Salt & pepper to taste
¼ cup grated parmesan cheese

Start with the recipe, a dingy yellowed index card transcribed in your own hand at some point in the last—what?—fifteen years, probably. Place it on the counter, read it over, and realize that what you have is only the ingredient list, not the instructions for putting the dish together. Tell yourself you watched your grandfather stand at the stove in their Florida kitchen and make these enough times that you can easily wing it. Remember, though, that he had your grandmother as his "wingman," so call your husband in and ask him to stand by.

First, make the batter. Beat the eggs in a gleaming silver bowl with your mother's red silicone whisk. Add milk and wonder if it's too much—it's not. It's supposed to be loose and thin. Add salt and flour, a little at a time, so as to avoid making a mess of lumps.

Or, dump in all the flour at once and curse when you see tiny islands of white floating on an eggy-milk sea. Whisk and whisk and whisk. Decide islands are nice and move on to make the filling. Combine all the filling ingredients and stop yourself from adding dried oregano and garlic powder, even though you are certain it would complement the cheese. Stop yourself because you want to honor your grandfather to the letter even though you are certain he wouldn't *give a hoot, darlin'*. He'd just be happy you're having fun in the kitchen, touched that you would take up his signature dish.

Think now, about the kitchen. This one belongs to your mom, who lives on the east coast of Florida, three hours straight across from your grandparents' home in Port Charlotte, on the west coast. This one is white and red and bright with new appliances. That one is seventies-yellow with worn linoleum and butterfly adorned dishtowels, pilled from years of use.

Or, it *was*.

The kitchen is still there, of course, but your grandparents are both gone two years now and you are making this most iconic dish of theirs in tribute, through some tears and some shame. Tears are easy to come by—you are an easy cry. Shame, though, is new. Shame came unexpectedly a few days ago when you and your husband drove past the abandoned rambler on Quesada Ave. You needed to see it, you told him, and he understood. The only home that had been in your life for your whole life, mortgaged beyond its value in a terrible market, no one to take it on, gone now back to the bank which is too busy to deal with it.

Shame came when you got out of your rental car and walked through the scraggy grass to the screen porch and peered in to find the walls still appointed with your grandparents' things: a portion of the rubber inner tube your son used as a baby near the now-drained and scummy spa; a wooden sculpture of the California Raisin someone made for them in the 80s (which you always hated); the Pennsylvania Dutch Hex signs you gave them for their sixtieth wedding anniversary—one says their names and wedding date, one says "God Bless This House."

In the Fantasy of What Could Have Happened Next, maybe you felt a proprietary impulse rise like spa bubbles from the hollow of your chest and you pressed the button on the flimsy door handle and pulled. *Locked. Rage and need.* Maybe you pulled again and this time maybe it opened. This time maybe you forgot yourself, forgot you were not coming into your grandparents' home like you had for thirty years, but were instead trespassing on bank property. In the Fantasy of What Could Have Happened Next, maybe you found yourself standing on the porch, stumbling past the spa and yanking on the kitchen slider. *Open. In.*

Maybe you stood in your grandparents' kitchen—empty and moldy now—and tried to remember everything that ever happened there. The phone call you took from the financial aid office about your college scholarship. Your mother making coffee. Your grandmother lifting her skirt up to her knee to show off her "great gams" to your husband while the video camera records. Your grandfather standing at the stove making crepe after crepe after crepe, filling them with cheese, layering them with tomato sauce in Pyrex pans. Hours on end.

And, too, that last November: holding his soft, weak hands at the Formica dinette (in the kitchen in which he swears your father still visits him), while your mother talks to hospice. Remember how you told him his love of sixty-six years was gone.

In the Fantasy of What Could Have Happened Next, maybe you grabbed one of their juice glasses—the red, blue and yellow striped ones they sipped from with their pills every morning—off the counter and fled back to your rental car, hoping that anyone who saw also saw your sobbing, remembered your grandparents, put two and two together and forgave you your trespasses, absolved you in your shame.

Leave the screen porch, the scraggy grass, Quesada Ave, your grandparents' and father's graves just up the road at Restlawn Cemetery.

Leave the maybes, the fantasy and go back to your mother's kitchen.

Be sure to let the crepe batter come to room temperature before you attempt to cook. Pour a cup of tomato sauce into the bottom of a square baking dish. Heat an 8-inch non-stick pan over medium-high heat and brush generously with olive or vegetable oil.

Ladle ½ cup of batter (possibly less) into the bottom of the pan and swirl to coat. Cook until the wet top looks dry-ish. Carefully flip (they shouldn't be browned) and cook five or so seconds on the other side. Remove to a plate or clean prep surface.

Understand that you are probably going to ruin several of these at the start. The pan will either be not hot enough or not oiled enough or you will rip them upon lifting and will have to fling them, cursing like your grandfather—*Yer sister's got a big one!* —into the sink.

Now it's a dance: put a tablespoon or slightly more of the filling in a line down the middle of the crepe and roll it up. While you are doing this, ladle some more batter, oiling the pan as necessary—which will likely be often—as you go. Place the manicotti into the baking dish as you make them. Resolve that you will be standing at the stove, thinking of your grandparents,

Rocky and Josephine, your daughter's namesake, for a long time.

When all the manicotti are snug in their pan, pour some good red sauce over them and top with some shredded mozzarella. Cover pan with aluminum foil and bake at 350 for 30 minutes, removing the foil in the last ten minutes so the cheese can get all melty and nice.

Let it stand on the counter for fifteen minutes before serving to your mother, who cared for your grandparents in the eighteen years of their life between your father's—*their son's*—death and their own, and to your husband, who is very glad to have you sitting next to him at the table, and not, maybe, locked up in Fantasy Jail.

12

AMERICAN HOME
COOKBOOK

I am a writer and a teacher, but if I ever dream of another life, another career, it would be in the culinary arts. I wouldn't want to work in or own a restaurant—I no longer have the stamina to keep up with the long hours. Maybe catering though, or better still, I would own and run a gourmet market. There are few places on earth I love better than those dusty little cheese and condiment shops with their shelves and shelves of loganberry jams, walnut oils, bars of bittersweet chocolate, jars of salt-cured anchovies and briny cornichons. I can spend hours in the local cheese shop in my university town, chatting with the young women (they could be my students) who work there. On slow afternoons, they indulge my tastes with the many varieties of cheese in their cooler and resting in huge, pungent wheels on the back counter. One afternoon: Drunken Goat. Another: ashy French Morbier. Last week: Ricotta Salata crumbly and tart with a sliver of Prosciutto di Parma melting happily in my very happy mouth. I have neither the ability nor the desire to resist such things, and even in graduate school when my wallet was not full, my cupboard always was.

I am also a reader and collector of cookbooks. Though I love the freedom of just messing around with fresh, delicious ingredients and excellent new cooking equipment, I also firmly believe in following recipes. When I do, I think of the person (likely, a woman) who first created it: testing it step by step in her hot kitchen back in 1973 or 1952 or 1890. I feel, as I always do when I cook, like I'm talking with someone I really like.

When I was a child, my mother taught me how to cook out of her dog-eared and already yellowed American Home Cookbook. My first dish: scrambled eggs. I remember the crack of eggshell against the metal mixing bowl and how she taught me to add salt, a little black pepper, a splash of milk, and her secret ingredient, grated Parmesan, before scrambling. I made moist, tender eggs first because that is the way I was taught. Later, I would go through a stage where I disliked any kind of runniness in my eggs—no glistening curds in the pan and don't come near me with anything sunny-side-up—and would purposefully over-cook them until the edges browned nicely, or the yolk hardened to a thin, yellow line. I loved these eggs just as I had loved the first plate because they had been my creation. I never felt they were wrong or bad, just inventive. That inventiveness led always to a soaring sense of joy; a new understanding of myself and my world.

My father spent his fair share of time with the American Home Cookbook as well. He would sit with its denim-blue binding broken open on his lap in the family room and cruise through the recipes while watching T.V. He didn't cook much himself with the exception of the occasional weekend omelet or canned corned beef hash heated in a frying pan. Instead, he circled or starred recipes he thought looked inviting and passed them on to my mother who would then dutifully work to recreate them for him. King to royal chef. But my mother was the hand that fed my growing up, and she was, and still is, a good, generous cook. I could have bathed in her white clam sauce, and her crepe-style pancakes are still my favorite weekend breakfast.

Strange, then, that I should connect so many of my food memories to my father. Or maybe not strange since his scribbles and notes adorn my mother's cookbook far more than her own hand appears. He liked to be in control in this way and disliked being disappointed at table.

Brown food disappointed my father. I don't mean he

disliked walnuts or turkey gravy. I'm thinking now about a dinner we shared in our Connecticut home—these were the last years of my parents' marriage—with a friend of theirs, a young woman who had married one of my father's long-time friends. She had, by that strange mathematics that occurs when couples couple, become one of my mother's best friends as well. Liz was younger than my mother by almost fifteen years and childless at that point. She was fierce and a little snotty. I loved having her around because our usual rule of silence at the dinner table was waived when she joined us.

In this memory, my mother has worked to prepare something she believes my father will enjoy—rosemary rubbed lamb chops, maybe, or it could have been chicken Marsala, slippery with mushrooms and wine-sweet sauce. She brings it to the table with, I imagine, a combination of both pride (she knows she's a good cook) and anxiety (she knows she can never please him), and we prepare to eat. Side dishes: rice pilaf and buttered niblet corn.

"It's brown."

My father stares at his plate, fork poised, aggravated. Two words. I see my mother deflate, her shoulders slump, her eyes lose focus. She's gone without a fight.

"Corn's not brown, it's yellow," my sister counters. She is also fierce and a little snotty. "Mom, this is really good."

"It's all brown," he repeats. He's looking at her now, a look I remember as half smirk, half frown. I feel nervous and sick —*why does he always have to make her feel bad?*—and scan the faces at the table one after the next trying to figure out what I can say to save this meal, to make my mother feel valued again.

"Brown, huh?" Liz gets up from the table and goes straight to my mother's baking cupboard. She knows her way around this kitchen.

"You want color? Here. Here's color. Knock yourself out." She hands my father the green food coloring we use at Easter and at Christmas to color the egg wash on our cookies—the ones he eats by the plateful every year.

My father didn't say another word that night. No one did, but this time, the silence was different; this time it was full to bursting.

My husband asked me recently, "What do you like about cooking?" We have, for the last four months or so, been inviting a crowd of about ten people to our home for "Sunday Supper." This tradition was born for me not out of my own upbringing, but out of the meals I shared with friends at the homes of their mothers and grandmothers. For every stage of my life, it seemed I was involved in some way with a loud, quintessentially Italian-American family who gathered each weekend to eat "macaroni and gravy." Sunday Suppers, I realize, do not just exist in Italian homes; roasts of all kinds are carved every week after Mass and before football. This was not, however, something my family took regular part in, so I enjoyed the commotion where I could with the Napolitanos, the DeRosas, and the Romanos.

I love the idea of a simple meal: pasta, gravy, meatballs, bread and salad. A little wine. A little coffee. Maybe something chocolate or lemon for dessert. Add to that a mix of personalities and ages, some crayons and paper for the six-year-old artist among you, and you have my idea of a perfect Sunday. The thing that makes it more perfect still, is that I get to cook it as well.

So when I approached my husband about the idea, he was game, if a little hesitant. Ten people? Every Sunday? Won't that get exhausting?

No. Because the answer to his question—*what do you love about cooking?*—is everything. I could sit for hours (and do) with my cookbooks choosing recipes. I love the tedium of list-making and the companion project of inventorying my fridge and freezer to see if I still have chicken thighs, pork shoulder, and anchovy paste. I love wheeling my cart up and down the aisles at Wegmans' grocery store, picking out tomatoes for salad and peppers for roasting.

And oh, how I love the cooking itself. Growing up, somehow, I never learned to make a decent batch of tomato sauce. Let me be clear here and say that this is not my mother's fault —she herself makes wonderful sauce; I just never paid close attention to the steps. When I tried in my younger years, I always burned the tomato paste. I never got the seasoning right: too little oregano; too much salt. No depth of flavor. No complexity. So this year, for my own Sunday Suppers, I resolved to use my friends as taste-testers: I was going to nail the sauce once and for all.

And I did. Week after week I browned my meats slowly and caramelized my aromatic vegetables—celery, onion, garlic, and carrots for sweetness—then deglazed with good, drinkable table wine. I chopped parsley and basil and cooked my tomato paste just until rusty. Then I braised and braised and simmered and salted and tasted. Finally, I served it over my favorite pasta, perciatelli—long straw-like strands ("little garden hoses," one of my cookbooks calls them) through which you can slurp ribbons of sauce.

I have friends who say they have no appetite for their own cooking, that by the time the dish is finished and ready to be enjoyed, they've lost their taste for it. I am not that person. I am, instead, the person who takes a bite of her own food, and if it's good, proclaims, enraptured, "Oh my god!"

In my early twenties, when I was getting married for the first time, my mother tried to find me a copy of her American Home Cookbook only to learn it had gone out of print. Her own copy was both too worn and too valuable to her to part with. But two Christmases ago, she put up a search of online, antiquarian booksellers, and was able to find me a copy identical—but for my father's scribbles—to hers. I think of him now, my father, and see his swooping, insistent hand, the uneaten brown meal, his stingy, disappointed expression and his inflated expectations hovering there like a half-spent balloon above the table.

Just beyond him, though, I see my mother at the counter mixing dough for popovers—I know the way it will feel when I tear off the crisp brown top and let it dissolve, hot, against my tongue. On the stovetop she is sautéing celery in butter for stuffing; it must be a holiday. It's the best smell in the world, warm and sweet and green and generous, a suffusing smell that reaches me here, years later, while I flip through the pages and plan my next shared meal.

13

TWO SUICIDES

—for J. and G.

The Saltine is the perfect vehicle, the perfect balm. Humble and forthright, perforated for your convenience. What will you ask of it? Top it with hot butter and brown sugar caramelized into crunchy toffee. Spread thickly with milk chocolate, crystals of sea salt flecking the surface, sparkling like gems. Like life. Crush it beneath a wooden rolling pin and mix with cornmeal to bread banana peppers for deep fry. Dip it gingerly into chicken broth your mother brings to your room when you're fluish. Optimistically nibble during morning sickness, on the plane to Germany with your in-laws, the crumbs tumbling into your two-year-old's hair. He's in your lap, on top of your tender belly, stuck to his sister inside you, his long legs tucked up, for the next seven hours.

Simple cracker, think about buttering it. A sweet, creamy stick and a gleaming-dull knife in hand. In *Jim's* hand, that is, because you cannot eat Saltines without remembering him. *Jim, your once best friend's husband. Jim, your ex-husband's still best friend.*

Whatever else he was to whomever else, he was also, simply, your friend. There he is, in the living room, or the dark green kitchen of the apartment he shared with Kris, his wife and your best friend, in Hamden, CT, grinding coffee beans. You will drink it together from matching yellow earthenware cups. Jim made the best coffee you've ever had from a home pot. Saltines and butter were his favorite snack. Saltines are his body, dancing naked and unabashed in front of whomever, even you, with the heat cranked to ninety in the winter. Body battered by Crohn's Disease and diabetes, by a rotting, re-sectioned gut. Everyday pain. Saltines are his spirit, failing, a little further every day.

In Germany you nibble German crackers, something like Saltines, suck on crystallized ginger, break Unisom tablets in half and swallow them after your morning vomit. In this pregnancy, sickness extends past noon, assaults you in the car as your mother-in-law passes you air-sickness bags she has taken from the plane. It stalks you up the mountain roads in the Black Forest, all the way to the farm restaurant. Your father-in-law parks and you leap from the back seat, spring to the side of the barn so your son won't have to watch you heave, and up everything comes, again and again. When you are through, you laugh to find a thoughtful horse standing by. Her long muzzle close enough to stroke. You wipe your mouth and laugh. Go in and join your family for another lunch. Your body is good at this, you think. Since there is no foreseeable end in sight, you decide to embrace this as virtue. *Good job, body!* Some bodies can run, others fuck like fireworks. Yours knows how to purge itself. To cleanse. To emit. In Germany everything is covered with brown sauce and onions, and the asparagus is white and wormish, cooked to paste. Your son and husband eat wiener schnitzel and fries. You vomit crackers and ginger and Unisom. Fail to keep everything in.

It's Father's Day in Germany and you are all getting ready to go out for lunch to celebrate the men around you. In the upstairs bedroom of your husband's aunt's house, you check your email for the first time since being overseas. *Dear Sheil—* your former father-in-law writes—*this is a terrible thing to tell you over email, but I knew you would want to know. I'm writing to tell you that Gerry has taken his own life. I'm sorry. I know how much he meant to you. He swallowed a bottle of pills...*

Another friend. Another swallowed bottle. Eight years ago, in Connecticut, it had been Jim's turn. And nine years ago, you called the ambulance that saved him the first time. It was only luck. You were on your way out the door when he called, loopy from loss and managing real pain with pills. Not much different from every other conversation. Pleading and pitiful. You felt for him. Both of your marriages over. Both of you so broken and unsure. But there was something more than only broken in his voice that day. Something frighteningly sure. So, you made the call and he lived, achingly, one more year.

The year of your divorce, you are working at the coffee house, trying to save money so you can get back to school. Gerry sometimes visits you on shift. He has clients in New Haven. He takes you out for lunch to the sushi place on the corner of Whitney and Trumbull St. You let him talk because you don't know what to say, concentrate instead on ingesting the soft packets of fish dipped in soy and extra wasabi so you can cry in public and nobody will care. You are as mute as you were that night in tenth grade, in his basement, listening to Alphaville on vinyl, your eyes going wacky from red and green hexagons on the carpet. You thought it was a date, imagined he might want to kiss you, wondered when he would, but his questions were all about Susan.

You've been friends since middle school, right? Does she like U2? What color roses should I get?

Pink, you tell him. *I think she will really like pink.*

Gerry stands at the counter while you wipe things down, change the brew baskets, make mental check lists of all the things that must be done. He is dressed in his lawyer clothes, slightly rumpled dress shirt and tie. He always, even in high school, looked like a grown man.

Here, he says, and slides a plain white envelope toward you. *Susan and I love your writing. We love you. We want you to have this.*

You open the envelope and find a check for $500 made out to you. The memo line reads, *for grad school classes.*

The day you move out of the brown townhouse you shared

with your husband, Jim and Gerry both haul boxes up from the basement, help you collect all your pain, sort through your resentments. They let you cry but crack jokes all the while.

Jim calls you "Happy Pants" to taunt you. Walks into the bathroom while you are taking a shit. Laughs while you scream GET OUT GET OUT JIM GET THE FUCK OUT OF HERE NOW.

Gerry makes lewd jokes about your breasts. Sits across the table from you at the homecoming dance senior year and flicks spitballs into your Gunne Sax cleavage, henceforth to be known as Gerry's Favorite Dress.

They are not friends with each other, just with you.

You and Kris visit Jim's doctor together. This before the days of HIPAA, privacy being a concept far beyond you two couples who spent so much time in each other's company that friends joked about it being a group marriage. Weekends in their Westville or Hamden apartment, sleeping in the guest room. Sundays cooking elaborate brunches—you and Kris in the kitchen, Lyle Lovett on the stereo. Your ex and Jim walking the neighborhood, looking for newspapers but bringing home mangy-stray dogs instead.

Jim's doctor became a friend in those years of multiple intestinal surgeries, convalescence, constant pain-management, depression. He loved Jim just like you did. Loved his smart-assery, his largesse.

He means to do this, he told you both that day in his office. *He means to die, and I believe that he will succeed in spite of what we all wish, what anyone can do.*

You held hands, nodded your heads, knew he was right.

One Sunday morning, the summer after your husband leaves, after you move out of your shitty brown townhouse and into the basement apartment by yourself, Gerry calls you at seven, says, *Get your clothes on, Susan and I are coming to get you.* These days, you do what people tell you to do because you can't figure out what to do with your hands. You climb into the back seat of

the car driven by two of your oldest friends, now married for
five years, and let them drive you all the way to Newport,
Rhode Island for brunch. A three-hour drive and a two hour
wait later, and you are swooning together over pecan-crusted,
cream cheese-stuffed, maple syrup-glazed French toast. Overfull
of food and friendship and love.

Your boxes are all packed into various cars, the small U-
Haul you rented for the move. You tell your friends to leave the
Christmas tree, its fake brown bark and slicing needles, in the
basement for your ex or your landlord or for nobody. You don't
want it. You want nothing more than to see Naugatuck in your
rear view mirror, to steer the car down Rubber Avenue to Route
39—that road that connected your life with your husband with
that of your best friends, Kris and Jim, in Westville, and, later,
in Hamden. Jim is driving his own car—the red Honda you will
buy off of his sister after he dies—packed to the roof with the
stuff of your marriage, your sadness, your stupid, stupefied
hope. He leaves first, and you all follow, a caravan of expectation and resignation. Of *this is what it's come to,* and *let's get it over
with.* In Westville he turns left while you continue on to
Hamden. You don't know where he's gone, but somehow, he
beats you to your apartment, places pink roses in a silver vase
on the mantel. Welcomes you home.

You are almost divorced. Just waiting for the judge to make the
paperwork official, to give you back your last name. You cut
your hair boy short, buy your first pair of Doc Martens to wear
to work. They are dark green and let you pretend you are a tiny
bit punk rock. One day, you tell nobody and leave the café on
your lunch break, walk down State Street to Studio Zee. You
hand the man your wrist and ask him to ink you a delicate circle
of vines there.

To help me remember, you say.

Something green and growing. Something tender and
tremulous and alive.

. . .

It's early morning on some day you cannot name and the phone in your basement apartment rings and rings. You follow it finally out of a deep sleep. You had been at the hospital with Kris, sitting with Jim, watching him until very late the night before. It's your ex-husband or another mutual friend calling to say Jim's family decided to turn off his life support.

I'm sorry, Sheil, he's gone.

You throw on your clothes and drive across town to tell Kris. They are divorced but that doesn't matter. She was his heart. She needs to know, and you can't believe they didn't call her first. You knock and knock and finally she comes to the door, disheveled, cloaked in sleep and pre-grief.

Kris, you say. And she sees your face and you see that she already knows.

The day Gerry is buried, you walk the paved path next to meadows filled with German chamomile and green nettles, the evening light gold and glowing. Your son runs ahead toward the playground; your unborn daughter turns your guts inside out. So far from home, from Susan, your oldest friend, now widowed and worn, you manage to keep everything in.

The day Jim is buried, you sit next to Kris in church, hold her hand while his sister speaks about all the love in his life, all the pain and support. She looks right at you both and you feel broken for your friend, not technically a widow since their recent divorce.

But her heart, her heart.

Jim and Kris were divorced when Jim died. Gerry and Susan were separated when Gerry died. You think about how your mother and father were also divorced when your father died- not a suicide, but a shock, nonetheless-and you know that it does not matter. You think about the Roethke poem about his student who fell from the horse and died. The teacher's lament —*I, with no rights in the matter, / neither father, nor lover*—and you know that there are no rights and that there are only rights.

That *this* is your right.

You loved these two suicides and they were not your lovers

or brothers or fathers. The heart-shaped spray your mother placed in your father's casket that said, *from your loving wife.*

Categories do not matter. They are no balm.

You think of your ex-husband, who you no longer love. You chop onions and peppers for chili and think, unbidden, of his eventual death. You allow yourself to cry for him now and you know you will cry for him then.

You know that loving anyone—however long they stay, whichever way they leave—means you take them with you. You take them in.

It means you open yourself to grief—inconvenient, tender-green and tenuous. A delicate circle, always growing and alive.

LINGUINI WITH WHITE
CLAM SAUCE

Serves 4 people on their way back from something hard

1 lb linguine or other—what your daughter calls "slurpy noodles"
2 dozen fresh little neck clams or 1 can chopped
1 stick of unsalted butter
½ cup extra virgin olive oil

½ cup dry white wine you would be happy drinking
5 cloves of garlic, chopped
½ chopped fresh Italian parsley
Salt & freshly ground black pepper to taste

Put a big pot of water on the stove and don't forget to salt it generously, recalling the time you did exactly that, and how your children now say things like, "Remember that time you forgot to salt the pasta, mama? DIS-gusting!" This is about truth, not manners. They were correct.

Call your mother to make sure you have her recipe close to correct. Leave a message on her voicemail and realize the time —she might be at an AA meeting. But she'll call you back. She always does, these days.

Send your husband to the store for Parmigiano Reggiano that you forgot to get at Wegmans earlier today. Unlike your other favorite pasta dish, spaghetti puttanesca, this is a sauce that benefits from the sharp, nutty, dairy punch.

Open the bottle of Pinot Grigio you grabbed on the way home, and hope that it is drinkable. You don't know much about white wines—you've always preferred red– but your mother does. Or, she *did*. Pour yourself a glass and hit it with an ice cube.

Remember—you can't help but remember—how the sound of ice against crystal used to make you cringe. Home from the office on a weeknight, still in her heels and trench coat, she reaches first for the glass, then for the bottle, then for the freezer door. Clink. Plink.

Remind yourself that your mother has three and a half years sober and has become, for you, a lifeline. Sip. Breathe. Be grateful and go chop the garlic.

Ask your husband to take pictures of the food for you. Acknowledge that he is better at this than you are. Be at peace with this. Let go of control. Let them—the husband, the clams– take care of you this time.

Soak the clams in a bowl of fresh water in the sink. Something about how the fresh water irritates, forces them to give up their grit. Let them sit while you chop the parsley, the scent of summer green reaching. Think about how it is only February but the crocuses, snowdrops, and even the tulips are already coming up. Tulips! Your parsley overwintered, lush and rangy, last year. Imagine next year fuller, greener, even more.

Rinse the clams and place them in the bottom of your blue enamel Dutch oven, and cover with 1/2 cup of wine (which tastes just fine) a sprinkling of garlic and a full hand of parsley. Consider some lemon but remember that it will turn the garlic blue. Opt not to. You can always add it later. Color is important. Remember your father's problem with "brown food."

Cover the clams and turn the gas to high. Wait for them to release their juice. Just a few more minutes. Resist the temptation to lift the lid too much. Be patient. Be patient. *Soon.*

Listen for the opining of the hard shells. (Note here that you meant to write *opening* but why not be quiet and listen to what they have to say.) There is a kind of ticking sound, a whistling, coming from the pot. This will remind you, undoubtedly of lobsters and crabs in pots on the stovetop in Montauk during the summer of 1979. You and your cousin playing H-O-R-S-E on the hot driveway outside the bungalow. Burying him in sand. The way the ocean water broke over you, tumbled you, terrified, as you tried to reach your father, only feet from shore.

Clams do not have faces. Be grateful for that.

In your kitchen now, the smell of garlic and wine and sea.

When the clams are done, realize you don't know what comes next. Should you remove them from the shells and toss them back into the sauce or pose them, prettily, atop a pile of pasta? It doesn't matter. Make a choice and don't look back. Either thing will be delicious.

Melt a stick of butter into the still-simmering liquid. Taste it. Add some oil. Maybe some salt. Pull the tender clams from their shells with your fingers. Put one in your mouth and bite down. Feel it resist and then yield. Yield with it and try not to think of sex or of the way your sister refused to eat this dish as a kid, how you could gross her out—and did—by saying the words, "sloop and slide, sloop and slide." Now put them back in the pot.

Throw in the rest of the garlic, the rest of the parsley. Grind some black pepper. Taste it again and feel the spoon burn your tongue just at the tip. Your mother still hasn't called back but it's okay. It's also okay to worry a little about how she will feel reading this. Tell yourself that she will know this recipe is really a love letter. Tell your husband to put the camera down and open his mouth. When he tells you yes, he likes it, but he likes his own mother's version better, that will be okay too. A mother's love and all.

Serve in the shallow blue soup bowls his mother gave you for your wedding over slurpy noodles. Grate some cheese.

Squeeze some lemon over it if you want. What you want is a bowl of delicious swimming things: noodles, garlic, clams naked but for flecks of black and green.

What you've wanted from your mother for twenty-five years, you've finally, wonderfully, fragilely, got.

15

PIN THE SOLJE ON
THE BABY

Mount Rainier

I am looking out for mountains.

I am flying with my husband from our home in central Pennsylvania across the wide Midwest toward Washington State, where his sister and her family lives. This is my first trip to the Pacific Northwest, my first trip into the extended family's extended family, and already I feel overwhelmed and nervous. My sister-in-law married into a Norwegian-American clan, a family who celebrates the roots of their heritage lavishly with ritual food and dress. I have been told that they are many and they are vibrant.

Here on the plane, I press my forehead to Plexiglas and search through the clouds. I have never seen what my husband calls "real mountains" before, having grown up in the east. I am transfixed. Here, from so far above, the Cascades seem surreal. Snow-covered, immense and craggy, nothing like the soft green curves of the Berkshires.

Mountains.

And then, incredibly, *a mountain on top of a mountain.*

. . .

Pin the Solje on the Baby

At the baptismal celebration for my husband's nephew, Erik, the children take charge. They have arranged elaborate distractions, amusements, printed personalized table cards for the dinner feast: a stew of sausage and chicken, apples and prunes, an aroma swirling in the air above and between us. After dinner, we play "Guess the Erik," a game in which each adult is affixed with an index card on her back listing a famous Erik from history, and the details of his fame. This is a guessing game. Which Erik am I? The only way to divine it is to ask questions of the others milling through the room. "Am I living or dead?" "Am I person or place?" Am I inventor or musician or athlete or King or conqueror?"

On the wall of the living room hangs the outline of a child. Featureless and curled, it reminds me of a chalk drawing at a crime scene. Body-shaped. Only the adults are blind-folded. We hear the voices of children laughing below us, feel their small hands around our hips, spinning us round and round until our inner compasses go wild, snap, point us in all directions at once. Then suddenly we are stopped, righted, our feet dance drunkenly to stay rooted. The children push us toward the wall, screeching, "Pin the solje on the baby!" The *solje*, a cool round disk pressed into our palms. A button for the *bunad*, the traditional Norwegian dress. We are supposed to aim for the torso and imagine a line of glittering soljes from neck to waist, like silver stepping stones in a fast brook, a safe path to cross. We lurch forward, arms stretched in front of our blind bodies, reaching toward the hanging form. The children squeal, "No! Higher! Lower! That's his *head*! That's his *knee*!"

The Wild Chickens of Bothell, Washington

We decide to take the path through the woods into town. The November rain is light but icy, though the ground is not yet frozen. I try to follow the muddy boot tracks in front of me on the way down, grappling for a foothold in impractically heeled shoes. At the bottom we come finally to concrete—a bike path with the Sammamish River on one side, a wide green field on the other. My husband's niece, Kaja, races away from us, dashes into a mass of feather and wing. She flaps her arms wildly, screaming, "Chickens!"

Wild chickens, in fact—a colony that dates back 20 years or more. Tufted and brightly colored, some with tails as long as peacocks', they clearly own this patch of land. No one can say for sure how they arrived in Bothell. Perhaps they were once beloved pets set free. Now, here, they flock and preen and bully the ducks and squirrels out of scraps of food.

Seeing them out of their normal surroundings is disorienting, much like seeing your doctor in the grocery store or out with her kids at the airport McDonald's. One does not immediately recognize them as chickens. At once ridiculous and fantastic; otherworldly and unreal.

16

MOTHER-OUT-LAW

I don't yet know that I am pregnant as I stand in my ex-mother-in-law's kitchen, chopping celery and onion for stuffing and stirring flour into pan drippings for the Thanksgiving gravy. The slight nausea and brain fog I'm feeling, the irritation like an electric current zipping through me I attribute simply to nerves. This is not new territory for me, but a wholly new context. I know my way around this kitchen. I've memorized it, could navigate it with my eyes closed. I know which drawer holds the oven mitts, scorched from years of use, and which shelf in the pantry has the rolls of aluminum foil and cling wrap. I could grab you a mug from the cupboard above the coffee pot, refill the salt and pepper shakers and sort the everyday flatware from the fancy silver and put them back in their appropriate places. I could stack the white and gold Corelle dishes in the cabinet and the paper plates and napkins on top of the microwave. I did these tasks countless times between 1985, the year I met my ex-husband while in high school, and 1998, the year I divorced him after a disastrous four years of marriage. In the living room, my new husband, Paul, now sits on the sofa talking with my sister and my niece. There, I spent years eating potato chips with bacon horseradish dip, watching Brian Boitano's Olympic figure skating routine on repeat, mafia movies, and, once, during an especially long string of pajama-

wearing snow days, the entirety of James Clavell's 1980 minis-
eries, *Shogun,* on VHS.

Despite not being a part of this family in any legal way for
seven years, I remember and still know so much about this
house. For instance, the whoosh of the storm door being pulled
open, followed by the squeal of hinge as the heavy black front
door swings in. So far this morning, it has been quiet. My ex-
husband has not yet arrived.

It was my idea to do drive the almost 300 miles from our home
in central Pennsylvania to my old hometown in western
Connecticut, to cook the holiday dinner for my former family
because my former mother-in-law, Joan, was recovering from
breast cancer and couldn't manage it on her own. It was her
holiday and I knew she was struggling with the thought of
having to cancel it. I loved her and wanted to help. I always
wanted to help. Everyone, but most especially Joan. Also, my
new husband had not yet met my ex-husband, and for some
reason I thought this would be a good opportunity for that to
happen. (For some reason, I thought this was *supposed* to
happen.) In my most generous, optimistic heart, I thought,
"They are both intelligent men. Grownups. They will have
some things in common. It will be fine." When I suggested the
trip, Paul was game. When I asked if he thought he'd feel
awkward, he said "Of course, but that's okay." When I asked if
he felt jealous of my relationship with my ex-husband's family,
he said, "No. They are part of what made you, you." He's a good
man, and an introverted one, so I tried to make the trip a little
easier on him by promising,

"If at any point you feel uncomfortable, you can just get up
and go. I don't care if we're in the middle of dinner. Just go.
Take a walk down State Line Road and clear your head."

My ex-husband, I had warned him (and oh, he had heard the
stories), could be a bit... much.

Everyone else has already arrived. My sister, Catherine, and
her daughter, Lauren, have agreed to join us, partly because
they, too, had a strong relationship with this family, and partly

because they want to support me and Paul. I'm grateful for their presence, and remember rocking my niece, who is now eleven years old, as an infant in the thinly padded chair in the corner of the dining room. I have a photo of her as a toddler sitting at the table, striped shirt, someone's chocolate birthday cake smeared all over her face and a delicious smirk in her eye. This was a home for all of us.

"So, where is your brother anyway?" I turn to Scott, handing him a tray of stuffing for the oven. He's a cook in the Navy and it feels good to share the duty of the meal with him. When he was a teenager, he liked to put sixteen teaspoons of sugar in his coffee just to piss his mother off. Delicious smirk.

"Oh, you know Ex. He'll be here eventually."

I can feel a pulse in my teeth at this point, likely from grinding them in anticipation, when the hinge squeals and the door swings and Ex finally appears in the doorway. He is wearing black everything: black jeans, black sweatshirt, black boots. Is his hair still dyed black? I can't tell. Could just be the regular dark brown. Dark black sunglasses he does not remove. He is singing a Smiths song and crying.

Oh Jesus Christ. Breathe, Sheila. Keep it together.

My plan all along had been to remain calm, centered, safe in the knowledge that I am now married to the *right* man. But in that moment, I felt familiar, yet disproportional rage. I hadn't seen him in several years. We went out for lunch a handful of times after our divorce when it seemed like maybe we could salvage some kind of friendship, but soon I moved to Pennsylvania for grad school and such pleasantries drifted into the periphery where they have stayed. Still, I know this act, this drama all too well. *Of course,* he had to make a grand entrance. *Of course*, he had to perform. I knew I shouldn't take the bait, but I couldn't help myself.

"What the hell is wrong with you?"

"Lisa dumped me," he said.

"Who's Lisa?" I (shouldn't have) asked.

Lisa was his way younger girlfriend, and I was moved from mildly anxious into permanently aggravated. The small cluster of secret cells that would become my son must also have known this to be some bullshit and decided to raise the temperature inside my skin and make my veins itch. Now I was sweating weirdly as well as aggravated and nauseated.

"Ah. Right. Well. I'm sorry."

I pivot back around to check the bird and minister to the vegetables and think, *We have to get the meal on the table. I can't deal with his shit right now.*

In so many ways, I had grown up in this simple 1970s split-level house—white with black shutters—on Westview Trails, just a mile from the home I shared with my own parents and my sister. I met Ex when we were high school and remember my first visit to his house. His mother would later tell me I did not impress because I didn't look her in the eye when I said hello. Well, that's highly probable. I was timid and unsure of myself and most things and people. Aren't most 15-year-olds timid and unsure? Later, I redeemed myself by accepting a last-minute dinner invite, after Ex and I had finished making out in his bedroom, probably.

"You're welcome to stay and eat, but it's just beef stew," she apologized.

"I love beef stew!" I told her, honestly.

And that was it. She accepted me. Eventually, our relationship roles would include surrogate mother, friend, and ally against her son's poor choices—the poorest, she thought, being his skedaddling from our marriage after two short years to have his quarter-century crisis.

But before that, we ate a lot of stew at their oval dining room table. We ate platters of pork chops covered in Shake 'N Bake. We ate sauerkraut pierogis handmade by his Polish Nana years before Paul and I and our kids would move to Pittsburgh where they could be had any day of the week, any time of the day.

Today it was going to be the traditional Turkey Day fare and seated around the table would be my former family and my current family. Eight of us total, pretending all of this is just totally normal.

. . .

"Lauren, would you like to say grace?"

Ex peers expectantly across the table at my niece whose pale cheeks pink up instantly. I feel someone kicking me under the table.

"Uh, no thank you?"

"Okay, no problem. Then let us pray. In the name of the Father and of the Son...."

I watch, shocked, as my ex-husband, a lapsed Catholic and avowed atheist for the entirety of our relationship, makes a protracted sign of the cross and then bows his head reverently to say a blessing for "our fallen comrades," or something, being oppressed around the world. The kicking continues and I can see my sister is trying to choke back a laugh. Paul is to my right and I'm trying to feel for any waves of anxiety or despair coming off of him. Nothing. His face is neutral, but I know he must be dying. *I* am dying and I have experience with this. But he's putting up with this theater for me. I turn to look at him, my eyes apologizing. "Remember your pass," I whisper, and then we tuck in awkwardly to eat.

My friends didn't really understand why I continued a relationship with Ex's family. They worried, I think, that it would just end with more pain for me. Right after the divorce, his mother had grabbed me by the shoulders and said, "Too bad. I'm not letting you go." *Yes*, I thought. *I'm not letting you go, either!* My relationship with her had deepened and grown into a full friendship over the many years of shittiness with her son. During a good number of those years, there were the extra pressures of my mother's alcoholism, and later, my father's death, that brought us ever closer. It was Joan who helped me make the decision to drop out after three miserable semesters at the University of Connecticut, and later, who stepped in to take me browsing for wedding gowns when my mother was not available. On the inhumanly long, hot day in late July when my father was admitted to the ICU, ten days before he would die,

Joan led me into her bedroom—the only room in the house with a reliable a/c unit—pulled down the shades and tucked me into her bed so I could cry and rest.

That we would remain in each other's lives made sense to me emotionally, but also, I had a precedent. My mother had stayed an ersatz daughter to her ex-in-laws after her divorce from, and the subsequent death of, my father. My grandparents had known my mother since she was 19 years old. They weren't letting her go, either. She would end up caring for both of them until they died, 18 years after my father. Maybe my marriage didn't hold up to any vows we made, but my friendship with my mother-*out*-law (as I came to call her because it was funny and irreverent just like I thought we were) definitely would. She would remain so important to me that I would drag my patient, understanding husband and our someday-child into a space dominated by the emotional vortex that was my ex and our damaged relationship.

Paul seems fine. Quiet, but that's not a surprise. I know having my sister and niece there helps a little. He has someone to exchange glances with when it gets weird. And this sure is a trip full of weird. Like yesterday. When we arrived in the afternoon, we found our sleeping arrangements to be an air mattress on the floor of Ex's childhood bedroom. I remember the year we painted three walls dark grey, and one a deep crimson. These days it's filled with his mother's crafting supplies—yards of wire ribbon, unpainted wooden boxes, cinnamon brooms—but it used to have a *Lord of the Rings* poster on the wall. It used to have a child's desk with drawers full of baseball cards, 12-sided dice and *X-Men* comics. Where the small loveseat now sits beneath the window used to be a twin bed. It used to be that Ex and I, as teenagers, would have sex in that bed as quietly as possible with his parents just down the hall. I guess I felt like reclaiming that space and that energy, so last night, Paul and I had sex on that air mattress as quietly as possible with Ex's parents just down the hall. Outlaws.

Wouldn't it have been something to be able to say I

conceived my son while having sex with my new husband in my ex-husband's childhood bedroom? Too weird and perfect. Such a great story to tell and thank the gods I don't have to. I have the privilege of being able to muse about such things without much gravitas because I never had children with Ex. For years I watched my sister struggle to remain cordial with Lauren's father for Lauren's sake. I've seen friends work equally hard to mesh old lives with new. I could have had a totally clean break but instead I clung to this role as ersatz daughter. Before I met Paul, I would travel back to Connecticut several times a year to visit. My mother-out-law and I would go shopping for hours at the Danbury Fair mall, just like we used to in the 80s. Before Ex marries and has his own, his mother and I will pretend my children are her grandchildren. She will encourage them to call her Meema and I will make novelty mugs with their photos that say, "Special friend," or "I love you!" that she will put in the cupboard above the dishwasher. It will feel natural for years.

It's time for pie and coffee, and just as I had done for countless meals in the past, I push back from my place at the table and begin to clear away plates and cups. Ex gets up to help, too—something I definitely do not remember from our time together. It's not the only thing about him that has changed, apparently.

"So, hey," I say carefully. "Can I ask? When did you become religious?"

I'm trying to walk past him in the tight archway between the dining room and kitchen. It means I have to turn my body sideways because he's mostly blocking it. We end up closer to each other than we've been in years. It feels both uncomfortable and too familiar.

"What? Why? Don't you have a personal relationship?"

"I don't understand. Relationship with who?"

"With Jesus."

Before I can decide if I should laugh or quick hop in a time machine to unwind what I'm about to see, he is pulling his sweatshirt off over his head and facing the table where my sister, my niece and Paul must be as aghast as I am (I can't bring myself to look at them) to see that he has shaved a perfect cross into the dark thicket of his chest hair. To show us all how tight he and Our Lord and Savior have become? Did I look immediately away? Did I stare too long and stutter? I don't remember exactly. It was otherworldly. Shocking.

"Right. Okay. I see. Got it."

I mean, what can you really say?

I have told the story of the Chest Hair Cross many times to listeners who are always equal parts appalled and delighted by the spectacle. It's a fun story to tell. It gets laughs and *oh my gods* and loads of sympathy for me, the woman who lucked out of the wrong marriage and into the right one with a Saintly Man who agreed to share a holiday with his wife's complicated past. One friend even suggested we get rich by writing a television pilot based on this one escapade alone. There are others, I assure you. Your mouth would drop open to hear them.

It's a ridiculous image, to be sure, the chest hair cross, and part of me—the part that ignores what I teach my students about writing balanced characters—intends to render my ex ridiculous in the telling. But I also tell it to remind myself. It's a way of illuminating exactly why I am so relieved to be divorced from him, to not have had children with him. To know that any connection I keep with my past is voluntary, chosen. Wanted.

Lately, I've been a pretty bad ersatz daughter. I haven't called on holidays and birthday cards stopped years ago. I've been so out of touch that I didn't even know that my mother-out-law, widowed now for many years, met someone—a nice gentleman!—who loves her and makes her happy and is teaching her about beekeeping. When I heard, I cried. It's been thirty-five years since the beef stew dinner, twenty years since my divorce from her son, and fifteen since I felt the obligation to show everyone what a generous, well-adjusted, good person I was by performing in the Thanksgiving family drama. The truth is, someone else could surely have cooked the turkey that year. My former brother-in-law had it all in hand by the time I whisked my angst and anger into the gravy that day. My presence didn't make anything easier for anyone. Likely quite the opposite. And it was my and Paul's first major holiday as a married couple. We would realize my pregnancy just a week or two later. We should have stayed home and made our own tradition. I should never have put him into this odd, uncomfortable space.

I still love my mother-out-law. She gave me life-saving support when I most needed it. She loved me. I think maybe she still does. I hope so. These days, I'm completely out of contact with her son, and she and I interact at a screen-mediated remove. Maybe I don't trust myself to be close to her without dragging us both back into the old sadness. It's close to the surface for me lately as I am trying to write my way into understanding how I spent a decade of my life marked by it, lost in it. Maybe I'm just tired and busy and it's hard enough to maintain connections with my real family—my mother, sister and niece; my children, my husband and his parents, with whom I have a more typical in-law relationship.

But also, Joan has actual grandchildren now (a boy and a girl), a real daughter-in-law, and a son who is apparently happily married and enjoying fatherhood. Whatever my feeling about the toxicity of our marriage, his mother doesn't deserve to breathe in that miasma. She had enough of that back then. God, we all did. I want her to enjoy her life and her family—her son—without worrying about me. So little by little, I pulled back. I pulled out and away.

I don't eat much beef stew anymore, either. Paul and I are trying to be more mindful about how our choices can affect our health, our world.

Still, I mess it up.

(Still, I miss her.)

It's a change I never thought I'd have to make.

꧁ 17 ꧂

THE PRAYER OF KALA RUPA

***Monks of the Dip Tse Chok Ling Monastery in
Dharamshala, India***

———

*"Twice in my life I had the same vision, I was suspended in the center
of a sphere that was not a sphere, every point of it converged at my
head and my feet like the poles of a magnet. I felt the weight of the
Universe through my spine, it was not harmful but overwhelming.
And I heard a sound, deafening, the whole Universe's vibration. This is
the closest to that sound."*

— YOUTUBE USER, SOLNEGROLUNAROJA

"When it's ready, my body will just push it out."

— DAKOTA FANNING IN *WAR OF THE
WORLDS*, 2005

———

1.

I was pregnant with my first child. I was woozy and large, overheated under late July sun, under the heat of generation. I sought refuge in the cool dark of a theater with my husband. On the screen, a movie star, a family drama, an alien invasion. From the screen, a sound, a single, reverberating note to score the extermination of humanity. I was the center of a sphere that was not a sphere, and I was not even the center, but my child was. I felt the weight of him, suspended there. Invasion. The sound emanating from the screen's chaos, the expunging, fields of blood, bodies, my body, my body, through the filmic fear. It reached through the dark and found me, converged at my head and my feet, vibrated up through our two, tuned spines. It plucked me away from safety. It felt harmful and overwhelming.

2.

I was in labor with my first child. Earlier, there had been music in the hospital room. There had been my husband holding me, dancing to light notes and melody. There had been sun through the afternoon window, then slow laps around the square of the corridor, the center of which was the nursery. A walking meditation. Hours ticked, my water long since broken, but my body still in stasis, suspended.

3.

I was giving birth to my first child. When the induction began, when the chemicals flooded into my system that began my body's relinquishing of him, a sound also began within me. It filled me as if liquid and I its container. It was shaped and luscious and devastating. It was in my spine and also upon it. It did not begin softly, but as a long, low note that I was compelled to hold. My husband held my hips as I held my breath and pushed. I held my legs apart and pushed. I held the rails of the bed and pushed. I held my husband's hand. I held myself inside of that sphere. I split myself wide. It was not harmful, but overwhelming. The sound was like a vision. I saw myself both before and after, my child both inside and out. I held the long, low note, felt my vibrating spine, the weight of the whole chaos, melody and movement, landscape and field, my body, my son, our breath, my blood, my center, both rent and whole.

THE EYES HAVE IT

My son was born with saucer eyes, blue and unblinking. I had labored without much effort, really, up until the final hours, which were strenuous and thrilling and obliterating and fragmented and completely, finally, *whole.*

The moment I felt his impossible skull erupt from my body, my midwife commanded me to "reach down and touch his head." I remember shouting, "No!" several times. I imagine this was done with violent shakes of my head, the way my son now thrashes when he is finished nursing or when I come at him with the bulb aspirator. My midwife grabbed my closed fist and plunked it down, where it starfished against something gelatinous and pulsing, emphatically alive. "Now push!" she said, "Reach down, and pull out your son!" He was born that way: my fingers hooked beneath his armpits, waving with one hand to his father, his cord—the longest my birth team had ever seen— throbbing like a python. With him on my stomach in the next moment, all I could see were those two dark saucers. Blunt-blue and unblinking.

My husband and I both have large eyes. This is understating it. I was once asked by a well-meaning old woman if I had had my thyroid checked recently. When I responded no and pressed her for a reason, she explained, "It's your eyes, dear." We knew our son would likely inherit this physical attribute, but neither of us were prepared for his eyes: huge and beautiful and thoughtful. The eyes have it. Everyone says so: "Look how alert!" "What a wise, knowing face!" "What are you looking at, little one; what do you see?" My husband's father calls from his home in Solana Beach to ask us, "Are his eyes still popping out?" Indeed.

Look. See. Watch. Observe. Draw in. Glimpse. Witness. Absorb. Peer. Perceive. Recognize. Know. This is the language of catalog, of the entomologist and his careful, organized bug box, of the artist in her cluttered studio. It is the language of the writer, the counselor, the priest who absorbs the world and its attendant pain, love, fear, joy; striving to draw out meaning and under-standing—connection. These are the professions of the high-minded, the curious, the intellectually inspired. Wasn't I a little smug when I fell in love with a man whose other love was philosophy? Didn't I, even before my son was conceived, expect him to love language, to eat books the way I did as a child and still do?

Who first said the old, terrible cliché, "The eyes are the window to the soul"? I circle phrases like this in my students' essays, reminding them to "refresh their language." I balk at the too-easy description, the expected explanation.

But still, there he is: in my husband's arms, in the Barnes & Noble in our town. It's one of the earliest outings of his life— his two-week birthday—and already strangers are staring and commenting: "How blue! How big!" Already he is staring back at them with that other cliché, the "knowing look." Does he silently admonish all of us for coming here to shop instead of supporting the small, independent book seller downtown? Is he disappointed in the purchase of a bodice-ripper-beach-read rather than a classic? Even my best friend tells me now that in those first months when she would come to visit us, she would hold him and think, "Stop judging me, baby!" Everyone knows you can't read James Joyce in the summertime.

And now, here he is again: sitting placidly in his Pack 'n Play, salsa music beating from the cat hair covered speakers in our living room. It's day three of our eight-month-old's current nap strike. Those eyes are wide from exhaustion, rimmed in red, practically pasted open, dry and almost vacant, but still... there is something imploring about his look.

When I was newly pregnant, I had a fight with my mother-out-law in the baby clothes department. She had stopped to finger a soft, cotton onesie stitched with soccer balls. "How cute!" was all she said, neither offering to buy it nor entreating me to do so. I snapped in that moment, wondering aloud *why* we had to adorn our children (my son) in sports-themed clothing just because some archaic notion of gender decrees boys to be natural athletes. No. No footballs on my boy's butt, thank you. We'll wait to see IF he develops an affinity for such things before we brand him. Of course we will support his interests whatever they may be: astronomy, cello playing, chemistry, chess.

This position of mine, espoused loudly and with emphatic smugness, makes people worry that we will deprive our son of the toy balls infants need for development. People close to us have promised him that they will take him to a ballgame if/when we refuse to. I tell interested parties: don't worry; he has balls to play with, and, don't worry; we might even, if some dear friend were to buy us tickets and drive us up to Boston, take him to see the Red Sox play.

I understand why they worry. I have made a lot of noise about allowing my son to emerge from my body and into the world of his own tastes, interests, and refusals. And as a feminist woman who married a feminist man, I have felt fine, even justified and self-righteous, about using sport as the locus of my argument and my complaint. Not all boys are muscular, vigorous, hyper, pushy, aggressive, active—what my mother calls "all-boy." My husband was never an athlete. Chess club member? Of course. Creator of chemistry experiments gone awry? Absolutely. Bookish, shy boy with rich internal life? Yes, and how marvelous!

And what about genetics? I was the girl they stuck way out next to the church parking lot in deep right field; the one who let the volleyball bounce off of her head during gym class. "Squillante," they admonished, "don't be afraid of the ball!"

But over the last few months, as strangers and family

remark how "wise" our son looks, "how astute" he must be, and how he clearly must be "soaking it all up," "taking it all in," observing, remembering, witnessing, cataloging—and as I go along willingly and even proudly—I wonder why I am not also railing against the assumptions that go with this generalization.

The truth is that at eight months old, my son is not a passive observer. He is bountifully active: slapping me in the face while nursing, pulling my hair, sticking his fingers up my nose, climbing over and past me, so that he can gnaw on the seat cushion of my glider. He screeches, cries, and yowls. He whacks his open palm against the hard wood floors and against the skin of my chest as I hold him. He pulls himself up on every vertical surface in the house, lands on his bottom with a hard thump, pivots and is off again. His eyes are still huge, yes, and beautiful, but what of it? Does their size and seeming depth really incline him toward a scientific or contemplative or observational life? Not necessarily. But unlike my objections to people thinking of him, "Boy! Baseball player!" this assumption matches my own sensibilities just fine, so I don't spend too much time poking at it.

When I was seven months pregnant and feeling energetic still, before the long, hot stretch leading up to my son's August birthday, I shopped with my mother in the gardening department at Lowe's. We wheeled flats of petunias, impatiens, and pansies between the aisles and made plans to fill the back garden with bright spikes of color in celebration of summer and new life. At the checkout, I ran into a woman I know, another writer, whose son was then 18 months old. I asked, "How are you? How is S?"

"He likes to launch himself off of things," she laughed. "He cries when we bring out the books."

She blessed my blooming belly and we left each other, but her words stayed with me, spiky and stuck: *This is my fear*, I realized. That my son would be so different from me that some of the most elemental parts of my life—books, character, story— would be rejected in favor of something foreign and strange. That he might be an athlete, and I—the last-picked team member in elementary school, the adult couch potato—would hold him back with my own disinterests and fears. After these first intimate months in which our bodies have hardly been separate or distinct, I'm afraid that we will one day fail to recognize each other.

When I think about it on a day when I've had some rare sleep, when my head and heart are both clear, I realize that this is really fine. One of the reasons I love and am eternally fascinated by my husband is that he is so different from me. His interests and mine intersect in places, of course, but there are trajectories of thought and tangents of attention that are all his own. Much of the time I can learn only from watching him, but sometimes the watching is enough.

My son was born with saucer eyes, blue and unblinking, seeming to beseech from the day they opened onto my world. With them, he sees our cats clearly enough now to lunge for them, laughing, as they pass within inches of his starfish fist. He sees the Cheerios on the floor next to the plant stand with enough acuity that he is across the room and shoving one in his mouth before I can catch him. With those eyes, he spies me coming down our street on my way home from teaching each day. My husband holds him, facing out, just inside our screened front door. My son screeches happily, his strong legs pumping in excited punctuation. Before I can make out the deep blue I now know better than any other color, before I can see his face erupt into smile, he sees me—watching me slump under the weight of student papers; absorbing my relief at being done with work and on my way back to family; recognizing my face, my gait, my smile, my wave. He knows that I am his mother, and that we will reach out to hold each other in just another few, small steps.

❧ 19 ❧

CRY, BABY

I pull the car into our spot in the driveway, just in front of the ornamental grasses I planted to hide the water meter from plain view—a blight on the front of our none-too-attractive-in-the-first-place duplex. I'm returning from my weekly escape, the grocery store, with a bag of size 1 diapers and a large bottle of Extra Strength Mylanta—now an essential item in our medicine cabinet. The air is brisk and cold and pushes me toward the walkway and the front door. Before I get there, before I feel my arm brush against the dead brown fronds, almost as soon as I exit the door to the car, I hear it: the oven fan whirring at full speed in the kitchen. It is a sound that pierces right through any hide of optimism I might have grown while wandering the fluorescent aisles of the market, picking through winter produce and surveying the shelves of baby food, daydreaming about feeding sweet combinations of apple and pear, blueberry and oatmeal some bright day in the future. It is a sound that makes me freeze mid-step and tense from my brow through my shoulders and into the exhausted muscles in my legs, making it impossible for me to use them to bolt—a thought I have at least once a day now. It's supposed to be a sound that comforts, calms and soothes, an industrial shot of white noise. Instead, it has become the sound of futility and desperation. It's a sound that echoes in every room of our home and spills out the front door onto the walkway, into the driveway, into the car and all the way to the grocery store and back. It is a blizzard of sound swirling around me, numbing me, and behind it, over it, above it, all around it is the other sound: the sound of a baby screaming. Of *my* baby screaming.

I thought I could will myself to have a calm child this time. My first—my son—had been born with huge open eyes that seemed never to shut. My abiding memory of his infancy—birth through maybe six months—are of his eyeballs staring at me from every part of the room at every hour of the day and night. Friends and family who might have thought we were exaggerating our description, or that new maternal hormones were amplifying normal baby behavior for me, changed their tunes as soon as they, too, came under the searing gaze of The Eyeball Baby. When he did nap, it was for minutes, not hours, at a time. I remember a few years later, being at a party with some friends whose two-month-old I had seen picked up out of her crib sleeping, transferred to a car seat, driven across town, taken out of the car, brought into a crowded house full of voices and music, and passed around to cooing guests—all while she slept soundly. I was astonished and apparently my face said so, because my friend, Kim, who had seen at least half of this process unfold and who knew my son, looked at me and said, "No. You're not crazy. He *never* would have slept through all of this."

Though I said I knew it to be ridiculous at the time, part of me must have bought into the idea that all of my son's sleep problems were because my husband and I were nervous parents. When I found myself pregnant a second time I promised myself it would be different. I was so ready to be laid back and flexible. To let her cry for more than five seconds before leaping up to tend her needs. To avoid curtailing our social life because of her schedule. She can nap in the car on the way to my friend's house, I told myself. I was going to roll with it this time around. I had had a hard pregnancy—much harder than my first—with so much pain, nausea and discomfort on every possible bodily level. I fooled myself into believing my delivery and early days would be easier, *should* be easier. I had earned it, hadn't I? And everyone but everyone had told me: *second kids are easier.*

My writers' group is planned for a Friday before Christmas, and I am excited to debut my new daughter to the women in my life who have been supporting me through this pregnancy and who were with me through my son's infancy. I imagine it will be like when my son was little—she will smile, and coo and I will let her "aunties" pass her around while I munch pita and hummus and sip Mary's homemade lemonade. I am excited, a little nervous, but tell myself, "It will be fine. You can handle this." I figure if she starts to cry, I will just nurse her down, the way I did when my son melted down at a faculty party when he was a month old. No, it wasn't ideal or easy, but you do what you have to do and people just have to understand.

I walk in and everyone crowds around, peering in at this little person who looks so much like my husband that it's startling, a little unnerving. I pull her out of her car seat and lift her up. Almost immediately she starts to fuss, so I set myself up among the firm pillows on Mary's couch. Someone brings me a goblet of water and a plate of nibbles. I begin to nurse her and she eats for a few minutes and then pulls off. Her eyes are big, her face neutral. She is absorbing the room, the people. Aunt Kimmy wants to hold her and I am all too happy to hand her over. "Come here, baby," I hear Kim say, reaching across the coffee table to scoop her out of my arms. As I pass her over, her milk-drowsy eyes fly open and her face crumples into a sorrowful wail. It's almost exactly that fast. At first we smile and cluck and coo and say things like, "It's okay, sweetie" and "Mama's right here."

As we do, I feel smugly confident. Look at me, the seasoned mother. Unflappable. I am aware on some level that my friends are watching me. Marion, mother of five children. Judy and her two kids. Mary with her daughter, now grown and successful and off on her own. I so badly want to be as competent as I believe these women to be. I want them to see me as competent and more, even, than that. I am performing, I realize, when the cries turn to full-voiced wails. No problem, I'll just nurse her. She refuses. No problem, I'll just take her upstairs into a quiet bedroom—Mary's daughter's, filled with stuffed animals and sports pennants, artifacts from her growing up. "Poor baby," I say to no one. "She's probably just overwhelmed." I try to settle us on the bed, but she screams and screams and will not be comforted. I switch breasts. Maybe my let-down is too much on this side. She screams and screams. I try shushing. I try rocking. *It's okay, sweetie. Mama's here.* She arches her back and screams. I try to walk her around the room. She screams. Flails. Purples and reds. I can hear the voices of my friends downstairs, discussing Kim's poems and Cindy's memoir; Gabeba's travels and Judy's granddaughter, newly adopted from Ethiopia. Nobody is talking about the screaming coming from my child, though I am sure they can hear it, and I have convinced myself they are—no, not judging, not that, but *evaluating*—my ability to soothe her. Evaluating her temperament. Labeling her "touchy" or "difficult." She is not affable and social like her brother, who loved people from his earliest months. She is not a "good baby."

I am near tears now and realize that I need to leave. I am embarrassed that I've only been here for a half an hour and twenty-five minutes of that have been spent failing to calm my child. It's not that I had expected to be able to participate in the discussion, but I had hoped at least to be able to sit there with her in my arms, enjoying the clear winter light streaming in and the sustaining energy of these smart, kind women. I make my apologies, trying very hard to appear composed though I am indeed coming apart, and say my goodbyes while wrenching this stiff, wailing body into a car seat that seems, suddenly, far too small to contain her. My friends hug me and tell me not to worry. They wish me a Happy New Year and promise to call on us soon. The minute the door closes behind me and I mince down the icy driveway toward the car, I am sobbing with her. Both because I can't stand the idea that my daughter is in this much distress and because I realize that it's not my friends who are evaluating my performance, who are comparing my daughter to my son. It's me.

She is only a month old and the screaming never stops. We haven't had the presence of sleep-deprived mind to imagine this to be anything but, at best, an all-day version of the normal infant "witching hour," or at worst, a bad case of colic. But I'm starting to wonder. I remember these terrible crying jags with my son, the way my husband's "bouncy walk" was the only thing —short of my breast—that could soothe him in the late afternoon into the later evening. This time, my husband has actually given himself tendonitis from the non-stop bouncing and, when I feed her, it's the same pattern every time: suck hard, scream, arch and pull off, suck hard, scream, arch and pull off.

During the day she goes from quietly alert one moment, to red-faced shrieking the next. There is no lead up, no warning, no time for us to steel ourselves for the next round. It reminds me of the non-stop contractions during my first labor—like massive ocean waves cresting and drowning me over and over. We can create a pause if we take her outside in the frigid air— perhaps it stuns her?—or if we strip her entirely naked in the house. But it is *just* a pause, enough time for a quick, shallow breath before we all go under again.

By Christmas she has been tentatively diagnosed (based on observed symptoms only) with Gastroesophageal Reflux—a condition in which stomach contents are regurgitated back into the esophagus—and prescribed the antacid medication Zantac. Lots of babies have reflux, I learn, due to the immaturity of the digestive system and the muscle that marks the boundary between the esophagus and the stomach. For most, this amounts to little more than a lot of spit up. They're even called "happy spitters." They are messy, but not in pain. These babies rarely need medication, just time for their bodies to mature. My daughter is not like them. She never spits up and is always in pain.

By New Year, we've switched her to Axid, but neither of these medications are doing a thing. I am supposed to hold her upright for twenty minutes after each feeding, but she feeds constantly, so how to do this? Sometimes nursing soothes the throat, quells the fire. But sometimes it feeds it. We never know which it will be. Her voice stays hoarse from crying, and all day long we hear the terrible chirp in the back of the throat that we have come to recognize as the actual *sound* of the acid as it comes up from her stomach and then goes back down. She is twice burned.

I take her to the doctor at least once a week for the first eight weeks of her life. Each time I'm there I ask the doctor, the same woman who has seen us since our first visit after her birth, "Just tell me, is this normal? Is it really reflux, or does she have colic, too? Is this just her temperament? Because if it is, I just want to know that and get used to it and get on with parenting my daughter."

I am in tears during each of these visits, feeling like a brand new, first time mother who worries over every single hiccup. But I wasn't even that mother with my son, so who is this woman second-guessing her own observations and instincts? The white paper crackles against the cold table. The baby struggles in my arms, serpentine, as we sit there and I feel help-less, frustrated, exhausted, and angrier than I ever thought I could be at my own child.

"No," Dr. K. finally says, levelly. "This is *not* normal. At this point, she should be smiling and looking around. I've never once seen her smile in this office."

She switches us to Prilosec, which is expensive and not covered by our insurance, tells me to make an appointment to see a pediatric GI specialist, pats me ineffectually on the shoul-der, and sends us home. There we work to find the easiest way to dose a screaming baby. Hold her upright? Do it fast? Droplets at a time? Pin her down and stick the syringe into the side of her cheek while her mouth is already an open chasm of pain. Watch in horror as she chokes and gags and spits most of it back up.

We notice for the first time the commercials for antacids that feature happy little purple pills and cleverly animated fire-creatures dancing fiendishly but playfully in a cartoon stomach. How can anyone think this kind of pain is fun or funny? With each medication we try, the 5-7 day wait for efficacy is horrible, interminable. We pass the hours, days, and weeks bouncing her while sitting on the purple yoga ball under the maddening whir of the oven fan in the kitchen. One day, while my husband teaches his classes, my two-year-old son sits glued to episode after episode of *Blue's Clues* and *Dora*, and I bounce her for seven hours straight. We joke sometimes that with all of this bouncing, our abs ought to be rock-hard and fabulous, but what we really feel is shredding pain in our lower backs and numb fatigue in our arms and shoulders from holding her. We bounce and know that improvement, when it comes, if it comes, will likely be incremental, but still we bounce and pray for immediacy. We long for a switch to flip, to turn this unhappy child into the smiling happy imp we imagined she would be by now.

It has taken us weeks to get an appointment to see the pediatric GI specialist, and when the day arrives, I don't want to go. I tell my husband that I don't want to drive two hours with a screaming infant to be told that I need to be patient with the medication, or that—and this is really my fear—I am blowing all of this out of proportion. But we go because in the end I cannot abide the notion that I didn't do everything I could. Even if it is fruitless.

The waiting room is filled with colorful wooden trucks and blocks and beads I know my son would have loved, but he is not with us. We could not imagine wrangling both of them while trying to negotiate the doctor visit. I had been instructed not to feed my daughter for several hours prior to our appointment, and by the time we arrived, she was clearly hungry and unhappy. As I fill out forms at the reception desk, my husband walks her around the room, pointing out colors and shapes and the friendly expressions of the people sitting in the red and aqua armchairs. The receptionist hands back our insurance card and suggests, with a smile, "Feel free to nurse her while you wait." I want to scream at her; doesn't she know that I was instructed *not* to nurse? Doesn't she recognize how difficult it is for nursing mothers to hold off for hours? How painful that is? How frustrating when nursing is the *only* thing that calms your screaming kid?

"I don't know why they told you that," she smiles, arranging pharmaceutical company pens in a plastic holder. "The doctor can do the tests either way."

I can see that she is trying to correct the communication error and to reassure me. I can even see that she is trying to be kind, but my daughter is squalling and lurching in my husband's arms, and he is entreating me with his eyes to *Take her! Nurse her!* and I am snapping at him in my mind and maybe even out loud, *No! We've gone this long without and I am not going to screw up the chances that the tests won't be accurate!* and I am worrying that all those kind, friendly expressions are going to turn any moment into disdainful and chastising scowls: *Why can't you calm your own child?*

I have forgotten so much about "normal" life. I have forgotten, for instance, that my husband is my partner and staunchest ally in this swirl and struggle; that he is the one person who I am certain knows I am not exaggerating the severity of her symptoms. I have forgotten too that the people in the waiting room are also parents of sick children, and that the waiting room of a pediatric specialist is no place for any such judgment. I have forgotten kindness—to others, to myself—because every muscle in my body is in a state of constant tense and retract. I feel like a small, nervous animal, always readying myself for flight.

The doctor removes my daughter's diaper, explaining that she will need a stool sample to test for occult blood. This will tell us definitively if she has the dairy allergy which often accompanies and exacerbates reflux. I like this woman immediately. She listens to every detail we offer about the previous three months, while moving her hands slowly and deliberately across my daughter's small, naked body. She is not screaming for the moment but looking around intently. Her eyes are beautiful —huge and blue, just like her brother's. I hear the telltale chirp, and then the doctor's voice, "Oh, that's reflux alright. Unmistakable. And yes, I see blood. Not a ton, but enough. No more dairy for you, Mama."

Though I have just been handed a directive to cut major elements of my diet for the better part of the next year, instead of feeling daunted, I am euphoric. I've had enough of prayer. Here is something I can *do* to help her. Goodbye cheese. Goodbye ice cream. Nothing tastes as good as this news.

Incredibly and, I hope, prophetically, my daughter sleeps in her car seat the whole drive home.

She's up again. It's 1 a.m. or 3 a.m. and I go to her, grope from the door to her crib and feel for her warm body, scoop her up. She stiffens against me; there is no yielding. There is never any yielding. In the night, when she wakes, she wants the breast and nothing more. She refuses the comforting touch, the hand gently stroking her back to sleep. Lullabies sung quietly into her hair only enrage her. *Shhh, baby. Mama's here.* She refuses still, at six months, seven, eight, to be soothed by latex or silicone. No pacifier, no bottle. No formula. Only milk. Only flesh. Mine.

During these months, while the meds are still in flux, she nurses as if in defiance, as if she hates that which she knows will sustain her, all the while writhing on the pillow in my lap. I tell people that she "launches herself off of me," that I am sure she will one day dive to the hard wood floor and break herself. I laugh and call her my "Flying Wallenda," trying to equate this quality with freedom and brightness of spirit. But in the dark in her room in the middle of the night, I nurse her while I cry and cry and a feeling of rage so powerful pulses from me that I am surprised it does not light the room. I am doing all the right things: medicating her three times a day, reading the finest print on labels to be sure my milk supply stays free of all dairy. But this isn't getting any easier. I am exhausted, embarrassed, and always demoralized. *Why can't I comfort you? Who are you? Why don't you love me?*

I know I love my daughter; I just can't feel it. I know, looking into her blue eyes and at her face, which a friend has described as being made "of milk and light," that she is smart, hypnotically beautiful and clever. But that hot reaching feeling, as if my whole body is propelled, reeling, desperately toward her, is missing.

By ten months old we have the medication finally right. But *I* am still not right. She is not screaming anymore, but I still can't look at her and feel tenderness. I call a friend who has moved away.

"I miss you," I say. "I miss seeing you."

"What's the matter?" she asks. "I can hear something in your voice."

I spend a few minutes avoiding, justifying, and qualifying my response.

"Oh, things are okay," I say. "It's just... hard. You know. She's just a very spirited creature." I try to laugh it off, but she sees through me. She is a mother herself. She knows.

"Sheila, you've had a hard time. It's not been easy. No one thinks you should be laughing."

"I don't know my daughter," I admit. "I don't know who she is and it's unbearable." I can feel the rage and the despair erupting from me with the tears that are always, always ready to come.

"That may be," she says, "but *she* knows *you*. She knows that she can be what she needs to be, feel pain and distress and that you will be there. She has always known you and *that* is what's most important."

She knows me. I take these words and make them a mantra, a life raft, a buoy. They help me mark my long days with her, help me see through the fog of sleeplessness and rage. Therapy also helps. As does a diagnosis of postpartum depression and a smart prescription for anti-depressants. I have been here before. Many have been here before. There is real comfort in this knowledge. It's not a comfort I can *feel* yet, but it's a comfort I can keep close, the way I keep close the fervent belief that I do love my daughter, that one day my whole body will bloom into joy at the sight of her. It's abstract and insufficient and not at all what I wanted, not at all what we both deserve. But I'll take it.

Oh, my baby—I'll take whatever I can get.

AFTER THE VERDICT WE
WATCH FIREWORKS

It's the Fourth of July, and Lisa and Jody have invited us to their
home in Lemont, PA for a barbecue and a firework viewing
after the sun goes down. Central PA Fourth Fest is celebrated
as being the biggest all-volunteer fireworks display in the country. The area around Beaver Stadium is transformed every
summer on this day into a carnival world and throngs of people
flock to the parking lots and grassy spaces, de-camp the way
they do during football tailgates, partake of funnel cakes and
hot sausage sandwiches from food carts. Cold lemonade.
Cotton candy, I imagine. I've only attended properly once in
the thirteen years I've lived in State College, and that was
before I had children. I prefer to watch from a small distance,
at a remove from the chaos of the crowd.

Paul and I live in College Heights and have since we were
married. This is the neighborhood just north of Penn State's
main campus, across Park Avenue from the football stadium.
We rent a rather nondescript duplex among beautiful, perfectly-
landscaped homes owned by tenured faculty. It is one of the
loveliest, quietest and most sought-after neighborhoods in State
College, and we could never, ever afford to buy here. I often feel
like a fraud, an imposter as I walk the easy ten minutes to my
office in the Burrowes Building on campus, or the twenty feet
through my back yard into oak-shady Sunset Park where we

have had each of my son's six birthday parties. We are lucky to have found this space—it's big enough for our family of four and has remained affordable on our adjunct salaries thanks to a kind landlord who likes us. We are lucky frauds. We know this.

Every year, we have followed our neighbors, our kids decked out in glow sticks and anticipation, to the lucky spot on the edge of our neighborhood. We walk up Mitchell Ave., turn right onto Holmes Street, stroll in the middle of the road if we like— the cars are infrequent and cautious of pedestrians here—turn left into the dead-end on Hartwick Ave., cross the Dean's long tree-lined driveway, and plunk ourselves down in the field that borders the Arboretum, what is to my mind the most beautiful spot on campus. Fireflies and fireworks, kids thrilled to be out way past bedtime. The landscape suddenly stranger and more mysterious than it ever is in the daytime. Adults nearby but not encumbering. *Magical*, I think, though my son used the word "miracle," and maybe that's close enough.

Lisa and I stand close by, chatting and watching the girls run around the grassy field and fling themselves into the hose-cold water of the kiddie pool or down the plastic incline of the Slip 'N Slide. Someone– another adult—set it up too close to the blackberry bush and we worry that the kids are going to go flying into the thorny branches before they can stop themselves. *Be careful*, we caution them. *Don't sit on the edge of the pool, it could collapse under you. Only one person on the slide at a time. Stay where we can see you.*

We wonder—Lisa and I and most of the parents I know— about how much freedom we should allow our kids. How much supervision we should provide. We muse about our own 1970s childhoods, remember them fondly as filled with something like benign neglect. *Sure, we survived*, we say, *we even thrived. But this, this is a different time.*

Dave and Lori are here, too, setting up their camp chairs on the lawn with the many neighbors who are beginning to claim space for themselves and their families in advance of the spectacle we are all here to see. We three couples have five kids between us, all between the ages of 4 and 8. There are countless adults here, but this place literally belongs to the kids. The field is *theirs*. It belongs to their school—Lemont Elementary.

And that house right there? The one that sits exactly adjacent to the field? Whose windows overlook the swings and the monkey bars and the kiddie pool and the Slip 'N Slide and the blackberry bushes? That is Jerry Sandusky's house.

On June 22, 2012, former Penn State assistant football coach, Jerry Sandusky, was found guilty of 45 counts of sexual abuse against children. On July 6, 2012, I am writing this sentence and re-reading the news report from PennLive.com which breaks down his charges victim-by-victim, and the skin on my arms and neck is bristling and I am having a hard time keeping my eyes clear and my spirit from screaming.

Like everyone—every single person I have spoken to about the Sandusky child sex scandal since it broke last November—I am supremely relieved by the verdict. I don't personally know anyone here in State College or outside of it, anyone who is or is not affiliated with Penn State, who has not shared my revulsion, my outrage, my despair and shame during these long six months of uncertainty. I have heard lots of strident ideas about what should or should not happen to the university administration that was in place and, presumably, in a position to act early and decisively in response to Sandusky's behaviors and crimes; lots of opinions about what should or should not happen to the football program and Joe Paterno's legacy. I've even heard a fair number of thoughts about what ought to happen to Paterno's bronze likeness here on campus. I suspect Penn State is always going to have trouble resolving their (now) complicated relationship to the beloved coach. But no one around me, *no one*, is expressing ambivalence about this verdict.

We say, *Thank God* and, *Thank the jury*.

We say, *Thank the victims for their bravery*.
We say, *Finally, someone listened to the children*.
We say, *Justice is served*.
But our hearts are still broken.

It's not quite dusk. Someone has put a plank down and is shooting off bottle rockets and a small arsenal of other store-bought pyrotechnics. It's loud; my ears actually hurt when they go off. My kids are running around, weaving in and out of other kids, adults, jumping over blankets and skirting lawn chairs with sparklers in their hands. I am thinking about the post I saw on Facebook that cautions parents that the tip of a sparkler burns at 1200 degrees. I am thinking about July 4, 1978, when my young uncles—14 and 15 years old—lobbed smoke bombs over the fence behind our house in Lexington, Kentucky, igniting piles of dry pine needles. How they had to scale the barbed wire to stamp out the fire. Later that night, I let my own sparkler burn down too far and scorched the tender flesh between my thumb and forefinger.

Lori is looking for Ben. He's in a group of kids on the ladybug climber that really, to me, looks like a giant spider. When they climb onto her back, they are at just the right height to grab a low branch of the maple tree. It's the perfect swinging limb, and there goes Ben, his light body flying for a moment before he lets go, jumps to the ground, smiling.

We watch the kids take turns from a distance. Lori says, "He can't hurt himself, but I am worried about that tree..."

We are all terrified all the time. That is a primary condition of parenthood. Yesterday, my babysitter told me, "Josephine says a bad man lives next door to Sadie and Jolie," and I want to cry because it's true. Or it used to be, because Jerry Sandusky does not live in Lemont, PA, anymore.

. . .

It's dark and the fireworks are going strong now over the stadium. My kids have given out four canisters of glow sticks we bought at Target before the party. It looks like every person here is going to a rave. Neon green, yellow, orange and blue. Some of the kids wield them like lightsabers—good guys versus bad guys—others decorate their bodies with necklaces, bracelets and crowns. Josephine herself sports a yellow one on one wrist, a green one on the other. This is how Paul and I locate her for the next hour. All we have to do is find those bright circles swirling against dark sky.

I don't really love fireworks set to music or narration, but this is part of what makes the central PA Fourth Fest so grand and beloved. The local rock station simulcasts from the stadium, and we are treated to a visual display and a soundtrack of patriotic anthems, pop music and even a partial reading of the Declaration of Independence. It's all just a little too rah-rah for me. But I'm putting up with it, leaning up against Paul while he snaps pictures of the lights in the sky. My favorites have always been the ones that look fireflies or weeping willows. Elegant and graceful. Wistful.

Rudy asks me why we are having fireworks today anyway and I explain that it's our country's birthday, so these are like candles in a birthday cake. That satisfies him for the moment, but tomorrow he's going to press me and I'll find myself trying to explain the Revolutionary War to a six year old by saying, "The people who lived here wanted the freedom to live according to their own beliefs. They wanted to be able to make their own choices; to be happy and safe."

I don't tell him that fireworks are also symbols for gunfire and ammunition, emblems of destruction, metaphors for war. He is only six years old and right now, I don't even want him to know that war *exists*. I don't want Josephine to know that Bad Men live in beautiful houses in lovely, quiet neighborhoods and do things to unlucky children that make their parents entertain thoughts of great, raging, righteous violence.

. . .

It's July 4th, 2012 and the sky over Lemont Elementary School is lit up like a birthday cake.

We watch our children's faces glow, their eyes spark with awe.

We think about the ten boys who were so grievously hurt but who screwed their courage and found their voices. We celebrate them.

We ease back into our camp chairs and our spouses; drink beer and lemonade with our neighbors and friends.

We are here. We are here. We are here.

The porch light on the house back there is still on, but nothing, *nothing* is as bright as this summer sky.

21

TORNADO

When I was a little girl in Kentucky, younger than you are now, I shared a bedroom with Aunt Catherine, who was still a baby. Grandpa was gone on business and Grandma took us to the Gardner's house. They had a little boy who was my age, so we played in the driveway next to their garage. It started to rain, and we heard on the radio there could be tornadoes, so we went home. It was raining very hard and our lights went out. *I don't like that.* I know you don't. I stood in front of my bedroom window watching the sky turn a pretty dark purple. I couldn't hear birds anymore, but I could hear, far away but coming closer, the sound of a train. *Was that the tornado?* Yes. And then Grandma yelled at me to get away from the window. She scooped Aunt Catherine out of her crib. We didn't have a basement, so we had to stay in the hallway until the storm passed. It was the safest place. *Did Grandpa know?* Yes, Grandma talked to him on the phone, stretching the long white cord from the kitchen wall all the way down to the hallway. *What did she say?* I don't remember. *Was he worried?* Yes. I'm sure he was, yes. *Did the tornado come?* No, it missed us, but hit the towns all around. *Did the tornado come?* Yes, and Grandma laid her body on top of us as the house shook and shook.

22

NAMING THE PARTS

She's four and it's bath time. She loves all water, has no fear of it. Last year while visiting Oma and Opa in California, she stood facing the Pacific at sunset. A breeze skittered through the blond floss of her hair. Steady surf. I was watching her, in awe of vastness—that of my daughter, that of the water she was suddenly gamboling toward. She got as far as the edge where the sand darkens before we had her by her small hand. She sat down in the froth, delighted.

"Josie," I say, "go into your room and get ready for the bath. Mommy will fill the tub up."

"With bubbles?"

"Sure, with bubbles. But just a few."

I remember the carnation pink bottle of Mr. Bubble my mother would buy for my own bath times as a child. Or maybe I'm remembering a wish. How I *wanted* that bottle, with its suggestion of candy in both color and sweet bubblegum smell. When did I learn to be afraid of bubbles in the bath? Likely it was my pediatrician, Dr. Perkel, who said, "Soap is an irritant. Especially for little girls." Did he use the anatomical term? Did he say vulva? This was the late 1970s. I doubt it.

"In you go, little Shmoop," I say as I lift her into the tub.

Not for the first time, I marvel at the length of her. At her lithe form. She is taut as a spring. There is not an ounce of fat on this child. We used to call her "Abs of Steel" when she was a small baby, because she felt like she was made entirely of muscle. The bubbles form a thin shimmer on the surface of the warm water. She stretches all the way out, reaching her toes for the chrome faucet. She can just about get there.

"Okay, lie back now and let's get your hair wet."

"Can I play for a little while?"

She points to her basket of bath toys. An Ariel doll from *The Little Mermaid*, and some denizens of her Little People village. A blue plastic cup. I pull the small green footstool next to the tub and take a seat while she plays. There is no way I am going to leave her in the bath alone. When I was her age, my mother left me in my bath to answer a telephone call just a room away. Long before the days of mobile phones, ours was affixed to the kitchen wall.

"Sheila, I'll be right back. I'm just going to answer the phone."

"Okay, mommy," I maybe said, lying back so my head rested against the hard porcelain.

I don't know what lead me to think, as she took that phone call, *I know! I'll trick Mommy! I'll pretend like I'm sleeping when she comes back in!* I didn't understand, could not have anticipated, her response then. I was not a mother.

"Sheila?"

Her voice sounded higher, faster than usual. I had lain back and closed my eyes. I was "sleeping." *Shhhh.* I couldn't just wake up right away. It takes more than that to wake a person up. I would stay asleep for another little bit.

"Sheila! Oh my God! Sheila!"

I let this go on a beat too long. When I finally opened my eyes, when she had finally caught her breath, she screamed,

"You scared the daylights out of me! Don't you know you can drown in a teaspoon of water? Don't you ever, ever do that to Mommy again!"

Now I look back on this memory and cringe—no cringe isn't a strong enough word. I feel such deep shame that I terrified my mother sort of on purpose that I have carried it with me ever since. I am thinking of it now, as Josie dunks her whole head back and under the foamy water. She is an imp—much more so than I ever was. I could totally see her trying to "trick me" that way. I'm not going to give her the chance today.

"You ready to play Name the Parts?" I hand her a clean washcloth and help her into a sitting position. The idea is that I point to a body part, she names it and washes it herself. This is a step forward in hygiene development. A step closer to her being able to bathe alone without her mother worrying that she could drown.

"Okay!"

This kid. Always ready for any game, any fun. I point to her knee, poking through the foam.

"What's this called?"

"Knee!"

"Right! And this?" I point to her hip.

"Hip!"

"Yup. Now can you tell me what this part is called?"

I point to the space under the bubbles between her legs. It's important to me that she can name her parts correctly, anatomically. I refuse euphemism and I abhor infantilizing language like *jay jay, fairy, nu nu, tu tu, coochie, twinkle,* which are all alternatives that come up during a Google search. I want there to be as little shame around her body as possible. Something I am still struggling with as a grown woman.

"Vulva," she proclaims with wild confidence.

She doesn't say vagina! I'm so proud. The conflation of these two distinct parts of a woman's genitalia by, oh, everyone, frustrates me to no end.

"Okay, yes! Good. Now do you remember what the inside is called?"

She scrunches up her face with concentration. She's going to take her time and I am happy to wait for her. The teacher in me knows not to rush in to fill the silence after a question is asked. Let her work it out. She finally looks out at me with those clear blue eyes and says,

"Um...celebration?"

Celebration. Celebration? CELEBRATION! It's the Hollywood sign in my brain! It's lit up like a theater marquee! It's a blinking neon "open" sign in the front window of my amygdala! I want so badly to shout YES! CELEBRATION! That's it exactly! Sure, it's a euphemism, but it's also a poem, a prayer: *may your celebration bring you pleasure with your beloveds, their fingers expertly finding your joy. May you be strong and resilient, like celebration itself. May children, should you want them, should you have them, issue forth from your celebration as you did from mine.* Pleasure! Strength! Celebration! Daughter!

I don't say any of this, of course. It's not time for such enthusiasm, nor is it appropriate for me to laugh like I desperately want to. After all, this is supposed to be an anatomy lesson. Very serious. Much at stake. So, I turn my head for a moment to reset my face, before turning back to her.

"Not quite, sweetie. Want to try again?"

Another long pause.

"Connecticut?"

(Connecticut?!)

I grab the fluffy towel from the hook next to the tub and scoop her out. She's shivering because the water has cooled and she has no body fat. I hug her toward me and marvel at her muscles tensing and releasing. She's already itching to be on to the next thing. My verb-of-a-girl. Always going.

"Connecticut. Well, no. The word is actually *vagina*. But it would be nice to visit our friends in New Haven again, wouldn't it?"

"Yes! Mommy, I want to play with Bella the dog! I want a pink birthday cake! Singing hamsters! But not the big scary squid at the museum. I like the room where you can open the drawers and touch the snake skins and mouse bones though."

"I like those drawers too," I tell her, promising we can visit the Peabody Museum again on our next trip. "You always get such a wonderful surprise."

❧ 23 ❧

LUCID DREAMING

In this dream of my father, the first I've had in several years, I have been given word that he survives. Not—and this is different from other dreams of my father—that he never died in the first place, but rather that he did and was cremated and buried in a wall in Florida, as I remember, but has now, somehow, come back to life.

In this dream of my father, I am not exuberant, or ecstatic, but rather skeptical. Not two or even five or ten years removed from losing him; I am where I really am: a mother at middle-age, more than twenty years into a fatherless life. When I hear the news, in this dream, I think about my friend, Tim, who, in real life has told me that his own father, at the age of 92, has fallen and broken five ribs. I think about how likely it is that he will die soon, and I feel sadness for my friend at the hole I know will open up in him. I feel, though I am fifteen years younger, a mentorial compassion. *Here*, I think, *let me help you learn how to lose your father.*

In the dream, someone tells me that my own father—*my father!*—is alive in a Pittsburgh hospital, and contrary to what I believe I would do in real life, I do not immediately drive there. Instead, I think about his cremation, which I, along with my mother, sister, and grandparents, readily co-signed. I think rationally about how unlikely corporeal transformation would be from bits of bone and ash. I think about my father's body. My father's very young and sick body. Tim's father at 92 might survive his fall. My father at 46 did not survive viral microbes.

In this dream of my father, I am my most real self. There is verisimilitude that has been absent in other dreams. I worry about the icy roads, for instance. I check the weather forecast and consider postponing the drive to the hospital until tomorrow, when it's warmer, less treacherous. He's not going anywhere, I reason. I am 43 and aware, in a daily way, of my own someday death. Of the vigilance required in keeping my children safe, alive. I am three years from being as old as my father ever was. Sometimes in the mornings after I shower, I stare into the mirror, my hair slicked and wet and away from my face. I look at my forehead, the place on him that seemed the smoothest. Stretched taut across the virus. He never looked old. I trace my lines from brow to brow.

What do I believe? That my father was too young to die. Yes. But also that it was, in some ways that are hard to admit to, even now, a relief to be free of his scrutiny so I could make my own life choices. (We all know what I did the minute he was gone. We all remember the white dress and the diamond and the sad years he had warned me about.)

What do I believe? That my life is lacking something that only his presence could amend. My daughter writes letters to my father on his birthday, "Dear grandpa, I wish I could have met you but thank you for taking such good care of our family."

What do I believe? That my life is rich and full even without his presence in it.

The hospital in this dream of my father is brick like Pittsburgh really is. When I arrive it is dark, so I must have braved the ice and cold. Yes, that makes sense. I would rush to him, wouldn't I? I would drive fast or fly, or I would even run. I'm telling someone in the lobby about Tim and his father, about the fall and the broken ribs. I am filling out forms at the reception desk, answering questions about death. *Year: 1992. Age: 46. Cause of death: Viral Encephalitis of Unknown Origin. Children: Two. Me and my sister, sitting in the ICU waiting room, waiting for our life to change.*

A man wanders by with a broom and asks me why I'm here. I tell him that I'd heard my father was alive again. That he was here in a room on the fourth floor. He sweeps and I tell him, too, about the icy roads and the brick and about Tim and the hole that's opening around or inside him. I leave the form unfinished (some questions are unanswerable), walk to the elevator and push the button. Doors open and I step through.

In 1992, automatic doors opened between the ICU waiting room and the nurse's station in charge of the patients' curtained quarters where machines beeped steadily or suddenly or not at all. I walked through them for ten days, in and out, in and out. Got coffee, drank it. Got food. Went home to shower and came back. Slept in hard chairs or on the floor, leaned up, achy and aching, against the wall. When I sat next to my father's bed, I stared at his smooth young face and shut eyes which did not move. I talked to him because I heard maybe coma patients can still hear you. I don't know any more what I said. I was twenty-one. It was a long time ago.

I have this dream of my father in Pittsburgh, Pennsylvania where I live, and it really is winter—the coldest I can ever remember—when I dream it. Ice glosses every surface, side-walk, road, brick home. I worry about my kids slipping on the crumbling front steps. One night the dining room windows crack clear across themselves from the cold and we tape them up. That's how cold I am, all the time, all the way inside me, into my dream and through to my bone. My father's real death happened in summer, in Danbury, Connecticut. I watched the sun come up that day. In an elevator in the hospital parking garage, an older (but younger than my father would be now if he had lived) couple had no idea. They smiled and wished me good day as they got out. The blunt bright seared the concrete rooftop and I squinted and felt heat and something else begin to fill me. The sky on that day, and for most years since then on that day, was the color of my father's eyes. The color of my son's eyes.

In this dream everything is brick and brown and my father has somehow returned from the golden fire of cremation. From the velvet box my mother carried in her lap on a plane to a hole in a wall in Florida. From two decades of gone. I hear whirs and beeping from some far off room. In my real bedroom, I must be coming out of my dream sleep, entering that place of lucid stasis, the space between here and there, then and now.

My alarm will ring soon, and I will have lunches to pack and children to ferry off into their day. I can feel everything starting. I am besieged by new urgency. I want to stay sleeping until we get to the fourth floor. I want to know if he heard me talking to him, if he felt me looking. I want to see. I will the elevator to ascend, the temperature to rise and rise, the roads to un-gloss and the windows to un-crack. I will myself to shiver and wake into the soft morning of a good, warm life.

24

CHANA DAL WITH RAITA

Serves 6 people at wit's end

1 1/2 cups chana dal
canola oil for frying
1 onion, chopped
3 cloves garlic, chopped
1.5 inch piece fresh ginger, finely chopped
4 cups water
½ tsp sugar
½ tsp turmeric

1 tsp salt plus to taste
1 tsp ground black pepper
2 tsp cumin seed
½ tsp anise or fennel seed
1 tsp coriander
½ tsp cayenne
½ cup shredded coconut
1 tsp ground cardamom
2 tsp ground cinnamon

. . .

First things first, go ahead and admit you are in a terrible mood. Really, just awful. Touchy and irritable, ready to banish any and all family members to the furthest reaches at the slightest affront. But look, take a deep breath and remind yourself that part of the reason you are doing this—cooking these meals, trying on the process of cooking— is because you loved your foodie father, gone now an impossible twenty-two years. It's because you miss him—an always-ache in your gut and your head like hunger—and despite the headache-inducing screeching sounds your children are making (and have been making all afternoon) from the other room, you love them, too.

Remind yourself that cooking usually makes you feel *better* and resolve to push through.

Check online for recipes. Read a few to get a sense of the basic shape of the dish and then decide to go forward with your own version. Recipes are good places to start.

Sort and rinse 1.5 c. chana dal in lots of cold water and put into a pot with 4 c. of water, salt, sugar and turmeric... except you don't have any. Dammit. Bring to a boil then reduce heat and simmer. Skim the scum from the pot of dal and give it a stir every now and then. Add more water if it gets low. Cook until almost tender.

Chop an onion the way you saw it done on a cooking show once—hold it down with one hand and make parallel slices through the half moon, then lateral slices down to create a fairly perfect dice—and remember watching those proto-celebrity cooking shows, the Frugal Gourmet and the Singing Chef, with your father on lazy Saturday afternoons.

Now remember him taking you to your first Indian meal in that restaurant in White Plains, New York. Remember the tapestries and brocade, the heavy shine of gold accents all around. How the air there was pungent and redolent, oily and almost unbreathable.

Invite your vegan friend to join you for this meal. Wonder what your father—glutton and lover of world cuisine—would have thought of veganism. Realize you know the answer but decide that he would have loved your friend– smart, wry, kind and curious– despite her dietary preferences.

Fry onions in three tbs. oil over medium high heat until they melt to a deeply rich brown. Every Indian recipe you've ever read has admonished you not to go too quickly, not to skimp on this step. Slow down. You need this. It will take more than five or ten minutes and will be worth the wait.

Chop the garlic and ginger and add to the onions once they have reached that caramel sweetness. Fry for another minute or two. Add onions, garlic, and ginger to the dal.

Pull the bag that holds your bulk Indian spices from the pantry and check to see what you actually have on hand. Ground cumin, coriander, cumin seed, ground ginger, some red-brown powder labeled, simply, "hot," ground cardamom, no fennel, but you do have anise seed which should work. Splay the spices and all the other ingredients over the single square foot of workable prep space you have in this kitchen (the last time you had an adequate kitchen, you were a child in your parents' home) and feel the walls close in. Unbreathable.

In a food processor, combine the coconut, cinnamon, 1 tsp cumin seed, coriander, cayenne and cardamom plus ¼ c. very hot water. Pulse into what is supposed to be a thick paste, but when yours turns out too soupy, remember that sometimes recipes are only good places to *start*.

Add paste to the simmering dal and cook for another twenty minutes or until dal is tender.

In a bit of oil, fry the remaining tsp of cumin seed and the anise for about a minute. Don't burn it. Add it to the pot just before serving. Taste to check spice level. Add some more cayenne at the last minute. Why not match the heat to your level of angst? If you overdo it, don't worry. There will soon be raita to cool all tempers.

Seed a cucumber and throw it into the food processor. Add a cup of plain yogurt, a handful of fresh mint, some ground cumin, salt and pepper. Process until smooth.

The kids will have stopped screaming, maybe, but they still won't eat this. (You didn't eat Indian until you were in college, after all.) Feed them bread and cheese and slices of orange pepper while you heat the naan and put some spinach or arugula in your mother's teak salad bowl. Its deep, elegant beauty alone could be enough to soothe you.

Let your friend, the vegan, keep the kids company at the table. Don't worry about how this recipe isn't perfect, how this day hasn't been perfect, about how your fantasy of a family weekend most always gets derailed sometime mid-day on Sunday. Everyone's screaming– actually or metaphorically– sick of everyone else and you all need to get back to your routine. Tomorrow.

Tonight, now, serve this dal over steaming hot basmati rice, topped with cilantro and drizzled with raita (spring green and tempting, even for a vegan) at the table. Pour a glass of chilled white wine, tell your husband and friend the story of that first rather mediocre Indian dinner with your dad, and really, just calm the hell down and eat.

25

STRIP DISTRICT MEATS

My nine-year-old son, Rudy, announces a desire to try turtle soup. It's summer and he's home for the duration. For a variety of reasons, we are not doing camp, so instead my husband and I are tag-teaming childcare and struggling to come up with fun/educational projects to keep all of us from climbing walls. For my part, I am teaching my son how to cook. It was his idea actually. At the library, we found a '90s Emeril Lagasse cookbook written for kids. He snapped it right up. So far, we've made Portuguese rice, Jamaican jerked chicken, BLT hot dogs with pan bagnat, and Caribbean roasted bananas, sticky sweet and caramelized with vanilla ice cream. He is learning to read a recipe, learning to read it all the way through before beginning to cook—something I have promptly forgotten to do twice during this project, despite having just schooled him on its importance.

We talk about the difference between the careful, devoted adherence to what's written and the pleasure (and sometimes peril) of "just winging it." I've been telling him stories about the people who taught me, variously, how to cook: my mother, my grandfather, my first mother-in-law whom we refer to as Meema. I use her as an example of strict adherence taken to an extreme. "We don't have cilantro for this dish, but that's okay," I tell him. "We'll just use parsley. Though if Meema were cooking this and realized she'd grabbed the wrong green herb, she'd abandon ship and order Chinese takeout." We laugh and chop the cilantro with the eight-inch chef's knife, my hand on top of his for the first few, sure strokes, then off. I feel a little bad using my former mother-in-law as a cautionary tale like this. There's nothing wrong with following a recipe, I say, but I want him to trust that he can improvise if and when it comes to it too.

I love cooking with Rudy. This has been the highlight of my summer so far. I am not great at structure with my family, not awesome at planning our long days together at home. I imagine other families, those better families, with their "staycations" or their "stay-at-home-camp" days: 8 a.m., organic, locally sourced breakfast; 9 a.m., organic gardening; 10 a.m., sun-hatted and slathered with SPF 70, hiking through the park before the blunt heat of day. On and on like this through the day, the weeks, the whole summer, in one-hour chunks of parent-driven enrichment. I have not pulled this off. I am either in my pajamas (and them, too) writing or answering work emails until 10 a.m., or else in my actual campus office while my husband, Paul, plays endless rounds of Mancala, Sorry!, and Monopoly with Rudy and his younger sister, Josie

But cooking I can do. The planning of it is pure joy for me. I love telling Rudy stories about my own first experiences in the kitchen, making scrambled eggs with my mother, or my first fine-dining meals—like the turtle soup he's heard me talk about and now says he wants to try—with my father. I also love that he seems drawn, as I am, to world cuisine and to challenging ingredients. I'm amazed that at this young age he appears game for almost anything.

In grad school I had a friend who said he wished that food could be taken through an IV or, better, a one-time injection. Nothing about the experience of eating brought him pleasure or joy. The entire process of shopping, preparing, and ingesting food stole valuable time from other things he wanted to do. His girlfriend and I would cook meals together in their tiny galley kitchen—roasted salmon, wild rice soup, Italian dishes that called for more garlic than seemed prudent. He ate and thanked us but never joined in our ecstatic feasting.

At seven, my daughter, Josie, has some of this. Except for sweets, her relationship to food is one of ambivalence at best, skepticism and disgust at worst. We used to say when she was a toddler that she subsisted on dust motes floating in sunbeams. Later, she will come to love pork soup dumplings at the Taiwanese noodle shop in our Squirrel Hill neighborhood and will ask me to teach her how to make scrambled eggs—the first recipe I ever learned from my mother. She will come home from third grade with a recipe for cucumber salad she learned from Farmer Tim, the instructor for the school's edible garden project. She will take great pride in her ability to execute both of these dishes by herself. "You don't have to hold my hand, Mama!" she will say when I try to guide the knife in her small hand. "Just tell me how to do it." Things with Josie get done in Josie's way and to Josie's own tastes: eggs cooked until they are a little dry, big chunks of crisp English cucumber doused with three times the amount of rice vinegar the recipe calls for. For now, though, she wants nothing to do with cooking and would happily exist on Double Stuf Oreos if we let her.

Sitting at the dining room table this morning, I sipped coffee out of my favorite yellow mug—the same yellow as the dining room curtains and the tablecloth, now pulled aside to let the light fall through—and I explained to Rudy that making true turtle soup might be difficult, given the illegality of turtle meat in some areas, but we can make a mock version. He asks how. I show him a recipe that includes the boiling of a whole calf's head plus brains. "Sure!" he says. "Absolutely. Let's do it." I feel a thrill of electricity and possibility. A powerful surge of nostalgia. *Yes, let's do it!* I make a mental note to ask my local foodie friends where, in Pittsburgh, I might source calves' brains, though in truth I'm not sure I could bring myself to prepare them.

The next day, I make fried cod for dinner, and despite my exuberance for the dish (crispy, not greasy, served with a cabbage and apple coleslaw I know he would love) he will not touch it. I say, "You'll eat brains but not fried fish? You know you're a little weird, right?"

"I'm not weird, Mama," he corrects. "I'm complicated."

It doesn't feel weird at all to be cooking with Rudy. Rather, it feels easy and pleasant and wonderful. But it does feel complicated.

I have been writing about my father and food since his death in 1992, when I was a senior in college. I have cultivated a large part of my identity around this eating, the conflation of his life-in-food with my own, and with the memory of meals eaten at his direction, in his presence, or his memory. Between my father and me, food was a shared language that stood in for other, more explicit modes of affection. It was also a site of great optimism (*if I eat this, I'll prove my worldliness, my mettle*), and anxiety (*if I decline, I will disappoint him, will lose his loving attention*). And now, almost twenty-two years after his death, I have this son, who never met him, who seems to be following in his foodie footsteps. But is he? Is he really? Or did I will this into being? Did I, am I, mapping this love of food—my love of food and all its complicated history—onto my son?

It's not as if I have a lot of evidence to present or ponder here. Rudy is only nine. Still, there was his Oma's guacamole, studded with fresh jalapeños, which he gobbled up at his first birthday party. There were the raw red onions he snatched off the falafel plate when he was three. There was the entire jar of chapulines—roasted, spiced grasshoppers—our friends brought back from their Oaxaca honeymoon. They were meant to be a joke, but when we unscrewed the lid and offered them, he grabbed them by the fistful, crunching happily and coming back for more. He had just turned four.

A few weeks ago, our family marked our one-year anniversary of living in Pittsburgh. To celebrate, we went out to dinner at a restaurant that overlooks Schenley Plaza. As always, we tried to find one that has a menu with enough variety to satisfy us all. For Josie, that means a cheeseburger. For Rudy, Caesar salad with crunchy croutons. Paul and I, craving a beach vacation that is just not within our reach this year, ordered oysters on the half shell as an appetizer. Six perfect, succulent mollusks arrived at the table, iced and glistening in their liquor, snuggled next to cocktail and mignonette sauce. Lemon wedges begging to be squeezed. Our favorite treat! *Three each*, I thought.

"Can I try one?"

Rudy stared at me from over his Caesar salad, and I honestly felt a proprietary pang: *These are* my *oysters! Get your own, kid.* But then, I remembered the vow I made to my father so many years earlier, which I have adapted slightly for my children: *Try everything at least once.* If they ask, when they ask, to eat whatever it may be (Fruity Pebbles; jalapeño chili dogs; precious oysters, quaveringly alive), I will always say yes.

"Do you want me to show you how to eat them?" I asked.

"No, I think I can do it."

I watched as he mimicked my motions, spooning a small drop of the vinegary sauce onto the shivering muscle, tipping the shell toward his lips. Swallowing. He's a quick study, my son. I watched for his face to shift into delight or horror, but he remained implacable. Only his eyes exclaimed.

"Well? What do you think?"

"Good. Can I have another?"

I traded him the rest of my share for his wilted salad. He slurped one and then another and then the shells were empty, the tray cleared away by the waiter to make room for the entree, whatever it was.

Later, he told me he had only eaten the oysters to make me happy. I was a little disappointed but not surprised. They are a challenging food. Paul says whoever it was that first ate a raw oyster must have been very, very hungry.

Already, at nine, my son knows that eating makes me happy. And he knows that sharing this experience with him in particular makes me especially happy. He's learned exactly the lesson my father's delights taught me. I don't want to push him the way my father would have pushed me. I don't want to make him feel like his refusal of food is a refusal of my love or affection. Every book I've read on feeding children implores parents not to "make food a battleground." So, I try to respond as neutrally as possible.

"No biggie, sweetie. It's great you tried it. Let's go see what Daddy's up to outside."

The local foodies come through with the info we need: Strip District Meats is our best bet for finding both calf brains and, it turns out, turtle meat. We've been to the Strip a couple of times with the kids already. While originally an industrial neighborhood, produce merchants and wholesalers took over in the early twentieth century and now it's a vibrant space for commerce of many kinds, but still mostly food. My children associate it specifically with the old-timey candy shop that plays the original Willy Wonka movie from the 1970s—the one I grew up with—on a screen in the back. Today, Josie has the hardest time choosing. She wants the foot-long Pixie Stix, but we steer her toward more temperate treats. This is a bribe; she has no interest whatsoever in the butcher shop we've trekked down here to find. She ends up with a small roll of Sweet Tarts, her brother with a package of Gummi Bears. We cross the street and head up the block to find the storefront.

It's Saturday, so the place is packed. I squeeze past customers leaving with packages wrapped in brown paper, into the narrow aisle between two long refrigerator coolers filled with meat, made even narrower by the crowd. I think the kids and Paul are behind me, but I'm not sure. I trust that they are and try to focus on the fleshy bounty to my right and left. There is every possible cut from every animal you usually associate with dinner (hamburger, whole fryer chickens, bacon) and those you might need for something a little more out of the ordinary (duck gizzards, beef tongue, hog maw). I scan the chalkboard menu carefully but cannot find turtle meat. I'm starting to think more practically about calf brains for this soup —or maybe oxtails would work—when I see that Rudy has gotten past me and is now motioning from what looks like an alcove in the back of the store. My first instinct is to chastise him for wandering into an employee's-only area, but then I see the freezers and the sign that says, "Exotic Meats." Okay!

"Rattlesnake! Camel! Woah, Mama, can we get some kangaroo?" Rudy reads the white labels on the boxes to me and I'm astounded.

I'd assumed Pittsburgh to be a meat-and-potatoes town, maybe a kielbasa and cabbage town, but clearly there are enough adventurous eaters in our new city to warrant an entire freezer of surprise protein. Who buys this stuff? The chefs who are responsible for the city's increasingly national food scene? I'm sure I've never seen camel on the menu anywhere, and I'm not sure I'd order it if even if I did. I can hear in my son's excitement both my father's influence and disappointment in me: *What do you mean you wouldn't order it? We had a deal, remember? You promised to try everything.* Or, more likely, he would have ordered for both of us and then fed me the camel from his plate.

In the end we leave with a pound of frozen turtle meat and nothing else, simply because I am so overwhelmed by the masses of people and the endless options. We walk back up Penn Ave. to the car, and Rudy seems excited. He asks me what other ingredients we need and I tell him I'll have to look up a recipe when we get home. Josie is positively horrified by the idea of turtle soup. She doesn't even want us to discuss it in front of her. Plus, she has an incredibly acute and easily offended sense of smell. I know that when I serve the soup that her brother and I will make, she will eat a peanut butter and Nutella sandwich, probably in another room.

If someone asked me about the most memorable meal I ever had with my father, I would likely say it was the one we shared on the college-visit trip to Philadelphia when I was seventeen. I would describe the fancy dining room, the candles, the turtle soup he ordered for us, and the warming sherry he taught me to add to the bowl. I would tell, again, the story of how he unexpectedly loosened up his normally serious and reserved persona on that trip, listening to pop and rock music on the drive and singing karaoke to embarrass and delight me at the piano bar after dinner. The taste of that soup has become rarified through time and memory and loss; I remember it as rich and hearty. I remember the meat as soft as braised beef and my father with a real smile on his face. How we enjoyed one another. It has been an iconic mouthful, a favorite memory of mine for twenty-five years.

In the kitchen, Rudy chops the mirepoix and I make the roux. After a while, it's time to eat. We sit down at the table, the bright yellow cloth lighting up the room. I feel happy. This cooking together has been delicious, but the soup itself tastes, if I'm honest, just okay. Maybe even slightly less than okay. The stew broth is thick and flavorful, but the meat—I could tell when I defrosted it—is very lean and sinewy and has a rather unpleasant rubbery chew to it. I hate to admit this, but I have to kind of choke it down with a lot of water—a technique Paul developed as a child when he was trying to break free from an unpalatable dinner quickly. Inelegant but effective. I try not to let on my disappointment, though I can tell that Rudy and Paul aren't enjoying it either. I want the spell to last, the circuit between generations to stay live a little longer.

With Josie in the living room, happily enjoying a bowl of Kraft Easy Mac and an episode of *SpongeBob SquarePants*, the rest of us each finish one bowl of turtle soup. While we do, I resist the urge to tell stories about my father. It's not easy. My instinct is to narrate, to fill in what I imagine to be missing. So much is missing. Years and years of meals my father might have shared with me and my children just for starters. But I keep my longing to myself this time. Maybe this uncharacteristic restraint will become part of Rudy's turtle soup story—if he has one—much the way my father's uncharacteristic openness was part of mine.

After dinner, I put the leftover soup into a container in the refrigerator. Maybe, I explain to Rudy as we clean up the dishes, it will improve over time, the way some soups do.

26

PRUNING THE FERN

The Boston fern hangs in the front porch the first summer my family lives in Pittsburgh. I buy it at Lowe's after noticing its pretty sisters in the doorways of neighboring houses. Calm and elegant, it turns slow circles in the breeze, against the dark brick, next to prim white impatiens and the leggy pink petunias that were my father's favorite.

Through the hottest months, I care for it along with the other new plants in my new yard. Stella D'Oro lilies and giant sunflowers obscuring the house's crumbly foundation. Bearded iris that sends up just one, tall spike so purple it's almost black. I imagine the way this one plant will spread in years to come if we let it. If we stay in this house long enough to see it.

Every morning, before the strongest sun, I go to my plants —I can't yet call them a "garden"—with watering can and confidence. I spray garlic and cayenne to deter bugs. I deadhead the annuals and give everything a good, long drink. I snip the singed tips of the fronds that strayed in their growing from the porch's shade. I tend to it and it grows gloriously green all summer long. But when the fall comes, I let it go.

———

I used to be a tender. I knew myself by this word and this action. People would ask me for help with emotions and green things. In graduate school, while housesitting, I got it in my head to re-pot all of my friend's houseplants as a surprise before she returned. I spread newsprint out on her small deck in the sunshine and one by one, loosed them from outgrown terra cotta, careful not to rip the roots. I spooned in dark, rich soil and moved them up to the next largest size, exchanging one for the next and the next until each had a new, roomy home. I used to think this was how I knew I'd be a good mother.

———

I stand in my kitchen on the day of the first snow and look out the window at the tall trees my neighbor and I worry will come down in a windstorm. Some of them are rotted, we've been told, and fragile. But the landlord says it's not his responsibility. The trees do not belong to him.

It's true that they terrify me—our kids play in the yard—but I also think there's great elegance in their flexibility. I like watching them. They bend far and sway, but, so far, stay upright. I don't know yet that this winter will feel and act three seasons long. Grey and relentless and colder than any other of my life, it will almost break me the way it will break my dining room windows, cracked through as if made of ice.

I've been depressed and the fern has been living on top of the book shelf in our front room, where we will put our live Christmas tree later in the month. It sits in a crumpled aluminum pan and I water it when I remember to. When I feel like it. I brought it in, optimistic, when the first freeze came, but by now it's more than half dead. Light as a breeze and browning steadily from tip to root.

———

Our last Christmas in our old town, we needed new lights for the tree. At Target, Paul and I let the kids pick them out, and they, being children, chose the rashly brightest, blinkingly garish, colored LED strands. I had my reservations. I may even have expressed them. But clearly, I was overruled. We decorated the tree and stood back to take it in. They were delighted. I was despondent.

For most of my own growing up, we had subtle white lights on our live Christmas trees. But when I was very young, I remember color on an artificial tree in our living room with the white carpeting and the gold and green striped couch. I remember sitting in my mother's huge wooden rocking chair with my knees tucked up under my chin, my feet bare against the cool, smooth seat. I think I remember Christmas music, but it's possible I'm filling that into my memory because it makes for a more picturesque scene.

What I'm sure about though, is that I was crying. I am sure that I was looking at that tree and feeling an inexpressible sadness that had, as far as I could tell, nothing at all to do with the lights on the tree or the music or the holiday in any way. I spoke to myself in my head: "Sheila, why are you sad? There's nothing sad about Christmas." It seemed ridiculous.

I was maybe six or seven years old, and when I think back on this now, I know with certainty that this memory marks the first recognizable moment of depression in my life. There have been many more moments since then, surrounded and informed by many different contexts, but the shape and timbre of the thing—the cold empty inside me—has never changed.

————

I'm alone in the house and can feel my mood collapsing in increments, the inverse of the snow piling up inch by inch outside. When this happens, everything feels like too much. The stack of unsorted bills and homework on the table, the dishes and cups un-picked up throughout the house, the cat boxes, the cats themselves.

In our old house, before we moved to Pittsburgh last year, every Saturday unraveled me. Something about all those hours at home without the structure of the work or school day, filled with domestic expectation, has always filled me with malaise and overwhelm.

I should be cleaning out the basement. I should be folding laundry. I should be enrolling my kids in music lessons. I should be teaching them how to ride bikes. I should be applying for better jobs. I should be exercising. I should should be writing. I should be able to snap myself out of this.

Instead, I do nothing but snap at everyone all the live long day. Paul says, "Mood colors world," and he's right. In despair everything takes on the color of a toothache. My therapist (#4 of my adult life), says, "Notice when you're catastrophizing. Interrupt your racing, negative thoughts. Find something to do with your hands."

So, I bring the fern into the kitchen and set it on the counter. Frigid air slides under the back door. It pushes through the poorly insulated outside walls, into the cabinets below the counter, spills onto my feet, which, like my hands, never feel warm. With the red-handled scissors, I approach my pitiful plant. I begin to cut away the dead bits. Some land on the counter, some float to the cold floor.

———

I used to be a tender. People, friends or not, used words like "calm" and "calming" to describe me. "Nurturing." "Motherly." I do mother pretty well. Well enough to see (worry, lament) that both of my children have tendencies like mine. A daughter who, at four years old, cried for so long and so hard about the loss of a grandfather she had never met that I thought I would never be able to settle her. Who tells me she "doesn't know why she feels sad, she just does." She writes him a letter on his birthday, and we plant his favorite pink petunias in pretty window pots. A son who, at nine years old, imagines asteroids, rogue planets, galaxies colliding with humanity in the impossibly far future. Who tells me he "can't turn off his mind." When my sister gives him a telescope for Christmas, he cries and cries and reminds me that he's terrified of space.

In the first year of my new job, the one that moved us to Pittsburgh, I would lie awake all night, and watch my own thoughts burst like constant, small explosions behind my clamped-shut eyes. My anxiety—*Am I good enough for this? Will the kids thrive here? What if I fuck this entire thing up?*—bloomed inside me and crept like vines around the room, snarling everything.

———

In the kitchen, the terrible fluorescent strip light—the one extra-shabby element of our new rental that I couldn't stop thinking about after we signed the lease, the one that made me want to cry every time I imagined living here—buzzes above as I cut and cut. It becomes obsessive. I do. I need this plant to survive. (I used to be a tender.)

The more I cut away, the more I want to cut away. I am surgical. Pull the lightest pieces away with my fingers, strip the fronds bare. I am surprised to find green fiddleheads, the tiniest furled shoots pushing through the thick tangle. Again with scissors I go in and trim close to the soil, except I can't really see the soil for all the debris. I consider getting tweezers to pick away all the dead brown leaves in between the fronds. I wonder if it's even possible to remove every single one. Maybe if I work in sections, I think. Maybe that would make it easier to tackle.

I try to work, but in this pruning, I've created a sharp spiky landscape that pricks my fingers. I am scraped and bleeding by the end, but there is clearly more green growing there and I must get to it. I bleed and laugh under a shitty strip light in a freezing kitchen, realizing this whole thing is an embarrassingly obvious metaphor that I can see, but will not be able to write about for another year, at least.

———

I've pruned back my life.

Where it used to be easy to tend my close up and faraway friendships, in this Pittsburgh year, it's become near impossible.

Where I would drive hours several times a year to visit.

Where I would mark birthdays with presents and calls.

Where I would look forward to socializing.

Where I would answer my phone.

Where I would call anyone, just to talk, ever.

Where, at the very least, I could write my way through dim and dark places.

———

Blood or no, I get scissor happy and, when attacking a thick, woody stem, slip, and a tender green shoot comes loose in my hand.

Shit, I say. And then, *I'm sorry.*

Because I'm aware that maybe this is not helping the plant at all. Maybe I'm even hurting it. But it makes sense to me that pruning would be a good thing—all the energy diverted back toward the vital essence of the plant. But I'm really no gardener. Surely there is a too-far here. Still, I'm tempted to sheer it all the way back the way our old landlord did every year with the ornamental grasses I planted to hide the water meter in front of our place. They always grew back, green and tall and lush, but it still hurt me to see them hacked to a stubble. There's something so elegant about those thin brown fronds, waving through the winter.

———

Every so often, I am tempted to sheer myself all the way back. Chop my hair off. Change my style. Do something extreme. People do this sort of thing to battle depression, don't they? But are those people really depressed? Bored, maybe, which can feel like gloom if it goes on long enough. Caught in a monotony of one kind or another. A pixie cut! A new tattoo! is just the thing to stir things up! I don't really believe these distractions will help. And yet, a faded vine of ink circles my wrist, a desperate gesture from the Zoloft days, right after my first husband left. I worried constantly. What would I do without his salary? I worked in the mall. How would I ever be able to afford graduate school? He had paid for my first night class.

How I worried and how I loathed myself, then. Could not imagine any person treating me with desire again. I laid awake nights and watched mind-fireworks exploding: *alone, alone.*

Looking back, I think my therapist (#1 of my adult life) was flirting with me. "You know, Latino and black men *love* women with your shape." But I couldn't tell such things then. I had no sure word by which to know myself. My sadness seemed like it could not fit inside my skin, even while I could feel it bumping against my bones. I gave myself over to his care because he said he would help me and I needed someone to help me. The pill he prescribed was meant to help quell my racing brain, dial down the constant terror and tears, lessen the lonely. Instead, it gave me crushing headaches and ruined my orgasm. We had talked about the possible side effects during a session and decided (*we? decided? how could I have agreed to this?*) that, "well, since your husband's gone, you're not having much sex anyway, so..."

———

That's one of the mind tricks of depression— you can't see the *whole* of the thing, only the garish, glaring ugly staring you down. You can't see, for instance, past the migraine-colored LEDs to the full green branches, or the strands of popcorn and cranberries that will later feed the birds. You can't smell the pine sap on your fingers or hear the bottom branches swish as the cats pass beneath them. You can't see the antique blown-glass moon your uncle gave you when you were ten, or the straw ornaments your father brought back from his trips to China when you were fifteen. You can't see the clothespin soldiers or the Santas or the hand-painted-by-your-own-kids angels—all of it dangling and dancing and dazzling right there in front of you.

———

The snow stays steady all day and the fern is not going to survive my efforts. Though I know this, I put it back in the Christmas tree room anyway. This time not on top of the bookshelf, but on a table right in front of the window. It will sit there for months and I'll continue to water it on Paul's insistence. I learned this part from him. He scolded when I put the petunias, spent at season's end, out for the trash. He refuses to believe a plant is too far gone to save. A year before we were married, we rescued a snake plant from the dumpster in front of his apartment. It was small and damaged, pretty pathetic, but my new meds were working, and I was a tender. We took it home.

———

When my first husband left, my therapist tried to convince me that my depression was only situational. He dismissed my childhood Christmas story as just so much nostalgia. He believed that all a young, beautiful woman like me needed was time, some movies with friends, more exercise, maybe some (orgasmless) sex. I'm not saying those things *didn't* help. But I knew, even if he did not, that it would get bad again:

Two years later, in graduate school, still grieving my father and worried that I'm

not smart enough.

Three years later, when another nowhere relationship ends badly and my father

is still dead.

Eight years later, post-partum and terrified with a new son and my father

is still dead.

Nine years later, on a sunny Saturday.

Ten years later, when I feel such profound disconnect with my infant daughter

(who will herself grieve deeply my lost father)

that it rearranges

everything
I have ever known about myself.

Sixteen and a half years later, during the longest winter of my life, pulling brown bits off of a dying Boston fern, making obvious metaphors and wondering if I'll ever feel warm again.

————

In a few months, just before our second Pittsburgh summer, the snake plant will send up greenish-white spikes of blossom in the light of the front room.

We will be so surprised.

We didn't know it could do that.

27

THE GREENLAND SHARK

Description and Habitat

Greenland sharks flourish in the waters around Iceland. They
move through the northern Atlantic and Arctic oceans, huge
and old and slow as mountains. Approaching the heft of the
Great White, they eat whatever they want—apex preda-
tor/crafty scavenger—and could eat you too but for the icy,
inhospitable habitat they prefer that keeps you mostly out of
their way.

Members of the *somniosidae,* or sleeper shark, family, with small
eyes and snub snout, underwhelming dorsal and pectoral fins,
they are less terrifying than awe-inspiring to behold. If you
beheld, which is hard to do because they can dive so very deep,
more than a mile, to hang out on the continental shelf.

The scientific name for the Greenland shark is *Somniosus micro-
cephalus,* which as far as I can discern, seems to mean sleeping
small head. Some call them gurry shark or grey, or by their Inuit
name, *eqalussuaq,* which just means shark.

My father was born and lived in New York for a lot of his life.
He died in Connecticut. Both states belong to the eastern

region of the United States, though in his businessman career, he did venture further east to Tokyo; as far south as Sydney and Buenos Aires; and West to Waikiki. In 1967 he left his hometown of Dobbs Ferry, New York for the northernmost place of his life—Anchorage, Alaska where he was stationed as an M.P. at the end of the Vietnam War.

Narrow-shouldered and slight, he nevertheless elicited terror or awe in my friends who would gather on our back porch under the ceiling fan after school. "Your father never speaks," they would say. "Does he hate us? Why is he always so quiet?" Holidays at my mother's sister's house, her eleven raucous siblings in the kitchen and my father, gone deep and solitary, escaped to the crook of the living room couch.

His name was Richard, which means brave power, but mostly he answered to *Rick*. His parents playfully called him *Churd*, which took me an embarrassing number of years to figure out.

Dentition

When feasting on the bodies of colossal prey—say polar bears —the Greenland shark's top teeth serve to anchor the animal while the bottom jaw's interlocking teeth cut through with a rolling motion.

When feeding on something he enjoyed—say sweetbreads or a greasy slice of New York-style pizza—my father would sometimes close his eyes while he chewed.

I find I do this while I brush my teeth.

History and Legend

Prized for their production of rich liver oil which was used for industrial purposes, the Greenland shark was once an immensely important catch for fishermen. In an Inuit legend, the first Greenland shark, a creature called Skalugsuak, is created when an old woman washes her hair in urine and throws the drying cloth into the sea.

My father never took us fishing as kids, but he told me stories about catching crayfish on the banks of the Hudson River when he was a teenager. I imagine him traipsing back to their dark railroad apartment smelling of stolen Budweiser and brine. His mother, who worked the night shift, would have been sleeping. If he was very quiet, he could sneak past without rousing her wrath.

Diet

The Greenland shark preys on cod, sculpins, lumpfish, skates and even smaller members of their own species. They scavenge seals. Parts of larger creatures like polar bears, horses, reindeer and moose have turned up inside their behemoth bodies.

My father's Army jeep almost hit a moose on an icy road in Anchorage. He told me it was one of the scariest moments of his life.

Anchorage and Reykjavik occupy almost the same latitude: 61.2181° N and 64.1265° N respectively.

In Tokyo he ate so much fresh fish. In Buenos Aires, steak—the best, he told me, he'd ever had. In Sydney, huge prawns, juicy with their heads still on. Good to suck.

In Honolulu in 1985, when I was fifteen and on a family vacation, we shared fresh pineapple until it shredded my mouth, and a surprising kind of seaweed you could pick right from the beach. Sweet and salty.

In Reykjavik with students in 2017, when I was 46, my father was not with me to eat *hákarl*—an Icelandic delicacy of fermented Greenland shark. To be honest, I had no plans of trying it, ammonia not being a flavor I want in my mouth.

Longevity

The Greenland shark has the longest known lifespan of all vertebrate species. The oldest on record is said to have lived for 392 plus or minus 120 years.

The current average life expectancy for a white, American male, like my father was, is 76.71 years. For white, American females, like I am, it is 81.48 years.

My father's life lasted 46 years and ten months.

I am currently 46 years and 8 months old.

Longevity in the Greenland shark likely has something to do with the speed—that is, the *lack* of speed, the slowest rate of movement of all fish species—with which it moves through the water. With only a top speed of 1.6 mph, even my father and I, so sluggish in the summer after his heart attack, could have outpaced it.

In this way, the Greenland shark is much like the gigantic Galapagos tortoise, *Chelonoidis nigra,* whose slow metabolism carries it forward, inchingly, on sturdy legs until it earns the word *ancient.* Wingless leviathan, it is quite the opposite, then, of the Ruby-throated hummingbird, *Archilochus colubris*, whose ceaseless, frantic flapping is fueled by a simple, evolutionary urgency: *keep moving.*

These are facts I learned by re-reading the essay, "Joyas Voladoras," by the writer Brian Doyle, who died this week at the age of 60, which is also much too young. I have a habit of counting up from 46 on my fingers, of looking into the faces of aging men and trying to find my father there. It feels wrong—voyeuristic and invasive, but the longing to know what he might have looked like at 50, 60, 70 compels me. I did not know Brian Doyle beyond his beautiful essays, but he had a kind, bearded face and a bright smile. My father, too, had a bright smile, though he was always clean-shaven. They seem to have shared the same preference for wireless-rimmed eyeglasses, though, and that detail alone is enough.

In his essay, Doyle observes about the hummingbird that "the price of their ambition is a life closer to death," and I think of my father's constant working, corporate climbing, always going, country after country, his never satisfied constitution or location, his not-presence, and I try, but no. I cannot find an analogous beauty there.

I have children, as my father did. If he was a hummingbird, then I will be the lumbering tortoise, the torpid Greenland shark.

Other Behavior

Greenland sharks migrate annually based on depth and temperature rather than distance, although some have traveled as far south as Cape Hatteras in North Carolina, a little over 3,000 miles from Iceland.

The farthest I'd traveled prior to my trip to Iceland was to Germany when my son was two years old. Since then, we have tried to take our kids to someplace new every year, though we haven't yet ventured that far from our home in Pittsburgh. Lake Erie. Washington, D.C. The woods of West Virginia. Iceland is 1,241 miles closer to Pittsburgh than Germany.

The farthest I'd traveled prior to Germany was to Hawaii for ten days when I was a teenager, 4,935 miles from our home in western Connecticut which was 7.3 miles from Danbury Hospital where my father would die 8 years later. He had won an award at work that came with a sizable cash prize, so we got to fly first class where they served us Dole pineapple slices and chicken Marsala on real plates for dinner.

As Food

The flesh of the Greenland shark is toxic because of high concentrations of trimethylamine N-oxide—a compound that helps balance the shark's internal salinity, and which degrades to become the characteristic stink of old fish—and urea, which is piss. In order to eat it, it must be processed by boiling and then fermenting, traditionally by burying in sand and gravel, for several months. The result is the Icelandic delicacy called Kæstur hákarl, or just hákarl, a foodstuff which even those two famous adventurous-eater guys on TV couldn't choke down.

"Mama, are you going to eat the rotten shark?" my son asked before I left for ten days in Iceland with my students.

And as I said, I hadn't planned on it. More than that, I had convinced myself that opting out would be just fine this time. I could watch my students' faces twist and grimace as they chewed. I could read the words they use to describe it in their journals on the plane ride home: *Windex. Old cheese. Feet.*

"Mama, have you tried the shark yet?" my son wondered every time I called home from Reykjavik because he is the child I have most closely shared this part of me, which was also part of my father: the curious, expansive, adventurous appetite that runs in our family. When he was two years old, he ate the raw red onions off of his Opa's plate. When he was three, fried, spiced grasshoppers from Oaxaca out of a jar.

In a few months it will have been 25 years since my father died, and it has always been that I mark that day with food I can imagine we might have shared. My father, in all of his global travels, never visited Iceland. Hákarl is something I know he never tried, and something I know he would have made a point to seek out. I have to eat the shark. I know I do.

So, on my last day, I wander the city, passing the souvenir-stuffed Puffin shops and window displays filled with scratchy-lovely Icelandic woolens, until I come to a tapas restaurant that includes it on the menu. The room is long and narrow with a warm wooden bench that runs the whole length and a wooden bar on the opposite wall. I sit by myself at a table close to the door and look over the menu of stained and stapled pages that lists various available bites: salt cod fritters, grilled lamb liver, sweet potatoes with vanilla yogurt sauce, licorice cheesecake. For 1600 Icelandic Króna, or about $16, you can pick four different tapas to start. That seems like plenty for lunch, so I place an order that includes the hákarl, and I add a shot of the caraway liquor called Brennivin, or "Black Death," that I've been told traditionally accompanies it. I've heard that you are supposed to dip the small pieces of fish into the liquor as a kind of seasoning. I've also heard what I expect is a more likely reason: you drink it down to kill the taste.

At the far end of the restaurant, a group of six young women, all with long blond hair, are celebrating a birthday. It's nice to listen to their laughter. White string lights over the bar reflect in the brushed chrome tabletops and I am at this point almost in tears from poignancy, thinking about my father and my son, about the power of memory and expectation. My food arrives quickly and beautifully in four mason jars on a wooden tray. I've chosen *acras*, or salt cod fritters, lobster soup with fresh sourdough bread, and beet hummus the color of crushed blackberries with celery pesto to buffer the bits of shark.

I've been gone for almost ten days and it's the first time I've been abroad without my family, the first time I've been anywhere requiring a passport in a decade. My father's job took him all over the world, but he never brought us with him. I always wondered if he missed us when he was gone. I guess I figured he didn't. I miss my family. I feel guilty that I'm here in this astonishing country without them, but I now understand the logistical impossibility of traveling with them, too. This makes me feel a little better about feeling left behind as a child. Iceland was a place my father missed in his travels, but here I am, these many years after his death, staring down three small skewers of pale, innocent-looking cubes of fermented Greenland shark, feeling his presence deeply and absolutely.

I raise the toothpick to my mouth and a jolt of ammonia hits me, clings to the back of my nasal passage. I have three elderly cats at home and this scent is familiar in the worst way. I push past it and take a piece of the fish into my mouth. One of my students recommended chewing it only for a few moments, as opposed to what she did: grinding it down to a paste in her mouth, allowing layers upon layers of funk to permeate and coat her tongue. I take her advice and bite down tentatively, noting the slight resistance—it's not as soft as sushi, not as firm as fully cooked fillets. I wait for the gag reflex I've been assured will come, but apart from a slightly sour, slightly musty taste, nothing much is happening. I sip the Brennevin and tuck into the rest of my meal, pacing myself before I'm ready to take another bite. In the end, I finish all three skewers of the shark because, why not? It's not delicious and I don't ever need to eat it again, but it's there and mostly inoffensive and I hate to waste food.

Do I wish it had been, as that famous adventurous eater on TV called it, "the single worst, most disgusting and terrible tasting thing," he'd ever ingested? You know, so it would make a more dramatic story? Not especially. It wasn't drama that compelled me into the restaurant, but obligation, which I had now satisfyingly met.

Conservation Status

The World Conservation Union currently lists Greenland sharks as "near threatened." Whereas in the 19th century, the sharks were an important commercial species for Iceland, these days most are caught accidentally in nets meant for other, more desirable species. And while it's true that hákarl has its roots in traditional Icelandic cuisine, it's now relegated mostly to tourists who seek it out to be challenged and say they survived. I cringe a little to admit to being that tourist. For sure this Icelandic lunch will take its place in my formidable food pantheon next to durian, the southeast Asian fruit so malodorous it's banned on public transit; and Japanese natto, another fermented food—this time, soybeans—whose mucous-like texture makes westerners (not my husband, but definitely me) shiver and squirm. I am at least part of the threat, but it's more than that, too.

There have been cultures throughout history whose funerary practices include endocannibalism, where family and tribe members consume the flesh or the bones of the dead in order to gain supernatural powers or immortality. The Wari people of western Brazil did so out of a sense of compassion for the deceased, a gesture of highest respect for them and for those they left behind. They believed that by ingesting the body, the soul of their beloved departed would be kept safely inside their own flesh, not abandoned to wander the forests alone.

I'm not going to tell you that I would have consumed my father's body after he died of viral encephalitis at the age of 46. But there is a part of me that understands how people did this, lovingly. I once wrote an essay where I said that I hoped my friends would consume my own dead body should our plane crash and I perish, yet they live.

My father was not a hummingbird or a tortoise. He was not a Greenland shark, swimming slow in the ocean or fermented and presented on a tourist's plate in a Reykjavik restaurant. Still, he is here, animal-shaped and substantial. Sour and surprising and also a little sweet. At home, when my daughter asks me where my father is, I always tell her, "he is in our hearts and our memories. He's in the stories we tell."

Yes, I carry him inside my body, in my gut. For 25 years, I have eaten his challenging, difficult love.

28

MOCK TURTLE SOUP

Serves you and your husband, his parents, your sister and brother-in-law, brother and sister-in-law, and seven kids (assuming they'll eat it), give or take.

3 large onions, diced finely
3 tablespoons butter; 6 tablespoons olive oil
6 lbs meaty oxtails
3 garlic cloves, mashed
1 1/2 tsp (or more) fresh thyme
3 fresh bay leaves from your mother in law's Southern California garden
3/4 tsp allspice (except you only have 1/4 tsp and there's no time to go back to Trader Joe's so you'll have to make do.)

3 tablespoons flour
9 cups hot water
9 cups chicken stock
2 14.5 oz cans peeled, diced tomatoes
salt and pepper
2 thin-skinned lemons, chopped finely (rind and all)
3 tablespoons fresh parsley

6 hardboiled eggs, chopped coarsely
Sherry, to taste, of course-ly

Think about the turtle soup you ate with your father in the fancy dining room of the expensive restaurant on the trip to visit colleges in Philly and realize that you will not be recreating it here. Gourmet though you may hope to be, you are a more ethical eater than he was or would be now, if he were still with you. Sea turtles are endangered even if you could find them. No, this soup will be an ersatz version.

The word they use is "mock," which is a word you always associated with your father. *I mock, you mock, we mock, she/he mocks...* or, mocked. *You.* At every possible opportunity. He was "toughening you up," he said. You who still cries so very easily, who has been called "ultra-sensitive," who, it must be said, passed this emotional tenderness on to your daughter. She cries when she misses her grandfather, dead so many years before she was born. She cries for hurt things and people. She cries for separations of every kind. You know she will cry and cry when her cousins leave in the morning.

Go in search of recipes online when you realize your cookbooks will be of no help. The first one you find calls for the whole head of a calf to be boiled down. No, of course you won't be making that. But if your father were here, if he were taking you into Chinatown, for instance, on one of your food adventures, sure you'd eat it. You'd relish its jellied weirdness. Think how you are cooking this for your father-in-law, one of the only other men you know who would swoon to dine on a dish made from actual calf's head. Head cheese. *Tete de Veau.* The rich pleasures of offal. You know your father would have liked him.

Instead, let your sister-in-law source oxtails for you. Listen to her call around to four different groceries and meat markets near Solana Beach where you are all visiting together– the first time in three years– and think about how lucky you are to have her support in all things– food and otherwise. She is someone good in your life.

Find them, finally, at Ralph's in Encinitas, and ask your mother-in-law to drive you there in the morning. She is all too willing. Foodies, everywhere.

Spend the rest of the morning suddenly worrying. (Foodies. Everywhere.)

Take a walk down to Cedros Avenue and buy some fancy olive oil for your mother-in-law, a butterfly garland for your daughter. Visit the store with the Provencal linens and fancy milled soaps you drool over every time and leave almost right away. Too much scrutiny, far too much expense.

Head back to the house with the jasmine arbor– still some blooms!– and pour yourself a glass of Pinot Gris, cold from the fridge. Pretend you are in your own kitchen. Feel competent and capable. Even more so.

Take the oxtails out of the fridge and sprinkle them generously on both sides with salt and pepper. Notice how beautiful they are. Like flowers– not tropical but just as exotic as the euphorbia and bottlebrush blossoms just outside.

Chop onions, garlic and parsley while your son and his cousin run in and out, arms whirling. Ask them what they're doing and when your son answers, "I'm not sure, actually," tell him he's in good company. Keep chopping through the onions' assault on your eyes, and as your husband wanders in reading to you from Lucretius' *On the Nature of Things:*

Then, further, we smell the various odors of things and yet we never see them approaching our nostrils, nor do we behold scorching heat, nor can we set eyes on cold, nor are we accustomed to seeing sounds; yet all these must of necessity consist of bodily structures, since they act upon our senses. For nothing can touch or be touched, except body.

Note your own body now, leg muscles aching from walks to and from house and hotel, from clutching toes hard to Pacific sands. Feel your shoulders tense– the space of strife, the stress of the semester still knotted about you like a shawl. Let them drop if you can.

Heat two large pots– the French blue *Le Creuset* Dutch oven that's just like yours but bigger, and the tall stock pot– over medium-high heat. Do half of everything in each pot. Add butter and olive oil. Add onions and brown them, stirring carefully and constantly. This will take some minutes.

Add oxtails and brown in batches, some in each pot. Don't crowd them. Add more butter and oil if you need to. Take them out of the pan and reserve in a large bowl.

Add spices and herbs, then stir in the flour until it bubbles. Don't burn it. Put the oxtails back in the pot and add the water and stock. Bring to a boil and then add the remaining ingredients, all except the egg and sherry. Lower heat and cover.

Simmer for two hours, then remove the oxtails and begin shredding the meat from the bone. You will mostly miss out on the appetizer of guacamole on the porch, but someone kind will bring you a chip or two and pour you some more wine. Add the meat— *oh! incredibly tender!*— back into the soup and reserve the picked-over tails. Think of your grandmother, sucker of knuckle and bone, and put a few small ones back into the pot. Treasures for the lucky spoon.

To serve, ladle soup into a beautiful blue and white bowl, adding chopped eggs, fresh parsley and enough sherry to make you glow at table.

Dip crusty bread and cut the richness— nothing ersatz here— with a fresh salad of greens, fennel and orange.

Toast your father's memory and accept your husband's family's compliments.

Be thankful for them, for sun, sand, water and breeze.

For body in all its manifestations, its various, complicated delights.

✧ 29 ✧

A STILL SMALL VOICE

"Mama, *please* can we go now?"

Rudy and I stand together at the shrine to Lakshmi, Goddess of Wealth, Fortune and Prosperity, but off to the side so that her devotees can pray unobstructed. Around her burnished silver form, a garland of pink blossoms; the ringing sound of worshipers chanting *vedas* lifts in the air all around us.

We have come as a family—my husband, Paul, and daughter, Josephine are behind us—to visit the Hindu temple in Monroeville, Pennsylvania, a few miles east of Pittsburgh, where we live. Paul sent an email a week ago, explaining that our interest in visiting comes from a respectful curiosity and wish to educate ourselves and our children about different cultures and faith practices. We were assured that visitors are not uncommon and very welcome. And again, we were assured, as we introduced ourselves to a security guard at the entrance, that, yes, it's perfectly fine to go in. We should please leave the camera outside and remove our shoes before entering. "We have coat racks down the long hallway. Thank you," he said, "for joining us today."

We learn from a woman behind an information desk that Ganesha, remover of obstacles, will be the first deity we encounter on our way up the stairs. This is a good place to begin, I think, as the kids are familiar with the elephant god. Before they were born, Paul kept a small silver statue on the dashboard of our very old car which sometimes started and sometimes did not. *Please remove this obstacle and let me get to work today.* There is a slightly larger, heavier figure on our fireplace mantle now, next to a similar figure of the Buddha and one of cheerful Budai, Laughing Buddha. In Rudy's room hangs a tapestry which depicts a Celtic cross and an Irish blessing; Josephine keeps her great-grandmother's rosary beads in her pink satin jewelry box. We are like a survey course in world religions around here. I like to think we treat all with equal measures of skepticism and awe.

There is a man in front of us who bows to Ganesha with hands pressed together in *pranamasana,* the gesture most westerners would associate with yoga mats and tree pose. *Namaste.* As he moves on, he reaches up to ring a heavy brass bell. Josephine stretches for the clapper—it made such a deep, beautiful sound—but I admonish her back. "That is not for us."

We climb a set of stairs to find a mezzanine where people chat and eat food which smells delicious. Almost everything is white—the ceiling, the walls, the thin January light coming through high windows. I wrap my arm around Rudy and guide him toward the central worship space, the *mandir,* I later learn it's called. I can feel him resist slightly. He turns his face into my side, and we walk in that way, together. We immediately move to the left side wall while a cluster of worshipers condenses in a strip in the middle of the room, in front of Venkateswara, a form of the god Vishnu, to whom the temple is dedicated. Almost right away, a woman wearing a deep red and gold *kurta* and a kind smile approaches me.

"Are you visiting?"

I nod. She looks around the room. We have to shout a little to be heard over the chanting. She points to the center space.

"They are washing the god now. You can watch. Is there someone here showing you around?"

When I explain that we are here on our own, she motions for me to follow her. This is how Rudy and I end up in front of

Lakshmi, listening to our guide explain the purpose of the bright red powder in the small bowl to the right.

"We take a pinch and put it here. "She mimics applying some to the middle of her own forehead, her third eye. "You can pray now here for happiness and health."

I am rapt by her explanation, grateful for some grounding in the moment and wishing hard that I had done some studying before we came. Rudy, on the other hand, is not rapt. Or rather, he is, but not with gratitude. At ten he already has a strongly defined sense of ethics. He is a rule-follower (like his mother) and becomes deeply uncomfortable if he senses things are out of their proper order or place. As we are, standing here in front of this foreign goddess, a family who has never attended any kind of religious worship together. The only white family, it also happens, in the room. I know this is how he is feeling because I am feeling it, too.

"Okay, honey. I think it's time. Yes."

I turn to Paul to get his agreement. I feel a little bad that we're leaving so quickly; this is something he has wanted to do for months. He teaches eastern philosophy to undergraduates and has always had a great interest in learning from these many traditions. But I sense that, like me, he is more concerned with not appearing like a tourist (which, I guess we really are) than he is with exploring spirituality today. We had wanted to educate our children, we said, and this had been a start. But now it was time to go. As soon as we exit into the brisk winter air, Rudy's shoulders relax and his facial muscles ease. He stops trying to hide in my coat.

"I felt uncomfortable," he tells us. "We didn't belong there."

We tell him that we understand, that the feeling is normal, even expected. This was a wholly new experience for all of us. These were rituals we had no point of reference for. We tell him we were a little uncomfortable, too.

"But you know," I say, "I'm kind of glad we were. It's good to feel a little uncomfortable once in a while."

. . .

It's lunch time now, and we head to a nearby Indian restaurant that has been recommended to us. We order an appetizer sampler and some dosas, and I pull a bag of cashews and a clementine out of my bag for Josephine who will probably eat nothing on the menu save for plain basmati rice. The food arrives and Rudy digs right into a savory fried cake, exclaiming "This thing is delicious!" and then proceeds to taste all the other treats on the platter with gusto. The food is familiar to us; Paul and I used to order huge samosas for delivery when Rudy was a baby and we felt trapped in the house. But since moving to Pittsburgh, we haven't had a lot of it. We've missed it. Josephine eats her clementine and sips a mango lassi. Everything tastes really good. We relax into the rest of the day.

In the car on the way home, Paul tries to lay out the basics of Hinduism to the kids. He explains the belief that there is one divine principle which takes many forms. At some point, Josephine interrupts his lecture (we are professors; it's what we do):

"I believe in God."

Oh boy. I think. *Here we go.*

"I don't," Rudy says. "That's just stupid."

This is not the first disagreement my kids have had about religion, but it is the same one they keep having. I find it fascinating, actually, that they've developed any religious faith (or lack thereof) without a church life or formal religious schooling. But here we are.

"It's fine to believe and it's fine not to believe," I say, "but it's important to listen and talk to each other without using words like "stupid," okay?"

I can't see what's happening in the back because I'm driving, but I imagine the look of resolve he gets on his face when he's ready to dig in. It's surprisingly placid, actually. Clear blue eyes. No furrowed brow.

"But I don't like it when people are wrong about things."

"I'm not wrong! *You* are wrong!"

There's nothing placid about Josephine's face, I'm quite sure. She is fiery in her devotion to an idea, this or any other, and just as stubborn as her brother. They are not going to agree on this any time soon. Still, I don't want to just drop it because it's difficult to talk about. I don't want to teach them that.

"Well, why are you so sure she's wrong? What makes you certain there *isn't* a god?"

"I just am. If you want to believe in something, believe in science, evolution. Believe in nature."

When the kids were two and four years old, we had a devoutly Christian babysitter and a cat who decimated wildlife. I was forever doing "carcass patrol" in the backyard before letting them outside to play, but sometimes, despite my vigilance, we would happen upon some small creature—a chipmunk or a vole—and play would pause so I could retrieve my gardening trowel and gloves. I'd scoop up the broken body and they would watch me carry it to the stone wall that bordered the woods behind our giant maple tree. We would stand together and acknowledge it—"We're sorry you died, chipmunk. We hope you had a happy life."—and then I would fling it into the bramble. I instructed our sitter to do the same.

At some point that summer, on a walk from our house to the park, Rudy announced,

"Renee told us that you have to die to meet God. That's where the chipmunks are now. With God."

I stopped pushing Josephine's stroller and turned to him, quite upset to learn my kids had been the target of a kind of proselytizing, whether well-intentioned or not. There seemed to be a lot of weight suddenly on the response I would offer.

"Well," I said carefully, "that's not what Daddy and I believe. We believe that if there is a God, it is all around us, everywhere. All the time. It's in the sunlight and the wind...."

"And the trees?" he asked.

"Yes, the trees. And even the chipmunks. In all living things. We think you meet God in life, not in death."

That satisfied him and we continued our walk, Paul and I and the stroller in front, Rudy trailing a few feet behind, dragging a stick along a dense hedge. We hadn't traveled half a block when we heard him cry out. We turned to see a clump of green leaves from the hedge strewn on the sidewalk at his feet.

"Oh no!" he exclaimed. "I broke God!"

My pragmatic secularist. My rational humanist. My ten-year-old atheist, who has grown from that moment to this one, firmly pushing away any notion of a divine creator.

"It's like Santa," he growls at his sister. "It's exactly like that."

And yet, he also believes in reincarnation and has since he was very little. Probably he picked it up from Paul's discussions of various faith systems, but certainly not because we espoused any particular idea of the afterlife. Rudy is an anxious guy and until very recently, his anxieties kept him from doing very normal things like ordering food in a restaurant or playing at recess with friends. It also kept him up at night, worrying about the expansion of the universe, the someday collision of galaxies, the possibility of rogue asteroid impact, and the eventual death of everything.

"The son of a philosopher and a poet," my friends would say. "What did you expect?"

For years he couldn't or wouldn't name his fears; he would only call me up to his room on the third floor, ask me to snuggle under the yellow fleece blanket and sit with him because he had a "bad thought." It makes complete sense to me that the idea of a soul having eternal lives would be comforting to his anxious mind and it also fits his budding physicist brain: the principle of mass conservation tells us that matter is neither created nor destroyed. It has to go somewhere, so why not into a new body? It's also so like the video games he plays too much of. You get to re-up your character after he dies at the hands of a bad guy or by falling off a cliff. You get to keep going or do it all over again. He used to tell me, "I'm going to grow up and invent an immortal potion so I can be with you forever."

Sweet. But now, his ideas are a little more complicated.

"Maybe we won't be mother and son in the next life," he muses. "Maybe we'll be neighbors."

"Yeah, or maybe I'll be a cat and you'll be a lizard!"

"Maybe I'll be a tree!"

"Maybe I'll be a squirrel!"

It's important to him that our souls (whatever we believe them to be, if we do) stay connected. He doesn't seem to care so much about the body.

His sister feels quite differently. When she was three years old, we climbed under the covers on her bed for stories before sleep. She asked me to tell her "Grandpa stories"—little narratives about my father who had already been dead for fifteen years by the time she was born. She wanted to hear them. She wants terribly to know him.

Grandpa surprised us with ice cream at the Red Rooster.

Grandpa brought me a squished marshmallow heart for Valentine's Day.

Grandpa ate all the Christmas cookies that were covered in glue!

I'd told these stories many times, but that night, for the first time, she cried. Actually, she *sobbed*, and *wailed*. It shocked me. It was as if she had known him her whole life. As if she had been there in the hospital room to see him die. My daughter was mourning.

Not long after, she began to talk about Heaven—the one that's an actual place sitting on a puffy cloud, where you can go and live in darling little houses and play on swing sets outside. Where people have their same bodies and minds and can find their grandfathers and ask them why they would ever eat cookies covered in glue. *That's just silly!* She believes she will meet him there, and that I will be there too, with all the chipmunks, to make the introductions.

And there was a time when I could have imagined that—the three of us laughing at his unlikely taste in sweets.

I was raised Catholic and for most of my childhood, took that very seriously, even grimly. It was impossible not to—my extended family on my mother's side included priests and brothers and nuns; my grandmother had gone the (only) other direction and had twelve children. My parents enrolled me in Catholic School, where we began every day with the Our Father and were offered the sacrament of Confession every Friday. I memorized and recited the Nicene Creed. I wore my scapular medal, inscribed with the words "Whosoever dies wearing this scapular shall not suffer eternal fire," under my blue plaid jumper not out of a sense of devotion, but, honestly, out of the abject terror of death. What if I took it off for my bath? Would I drown while my mother was down the hall in the kitchen, unaware? It was too much to risk. The itchy wool rectangles remained tucked under my pressed white uniform shirts for years. The same terror kept me from completing the bedtime prayer, "Now I lay me down to sleep," because it ended, I thought, with a ghoulish invitation: "if I should die before I wake, I pray the Lord my soul to take." No thank you. I was not about to tempt fate.

So, Catholicism scared me, but it also held me quite in thrall. Or rather, Mass did. I loved the sensuality of it all, though as a child I wouldn't have been able to name it as such: the smell and almost taste of particulate incense—frankincense —swinging from the priest's censer, the "kiss of peace" (my father's most hated part; "phonies," he would spit, and hold his arms tight across his body.), what it felt like to kneel on worn padding and, occasionally if we were very late in arriving, on the concrete floor of the sanctuary, which hurt, but my grand-mother told me that my suffering was a sacrifice to God and that I was fortunate to be able to give. I didn't dare complain; in fact, I rather loved the image of myself as a humble and devoted supplicant.

Most especially, though, I loved the intimacy of communion and the reflective time immediately following, when the church would be silent but for whatever hymn was playing and the soft shuffle of shoes making their way up the center aisle toward the priest. No matter what I had brought with me into Mass, what distractions, what annoyances or skepticism, and no matter how I tried to push my reaction consciously away, I would invariably come to tears during those few minutes. It was wholly beyond me. When I was a child, I would have been praying to be spared my own or the untimely death of my family. That certainly would have made me cry. Later, after my father really did die, on the rare occasion (weddings, funerals) I attended Mass, I was surprised to find that the post-communion reflection time could still set me to weeping, even without having taken part in the sacrament, or any part of the church or its rituals at all, for many years.

My leaving of the church had to do with dogma and rigidity, inequity and hypocrisy. It had to do with my own intellectual, feminist development and even, perhaps ironically, with the time I spent as a religion minor in college. It had nothing to do, that I can tell, with my father's sudden and premature death at the age of 46 from a viral brain infection the year I was set to graduate. Though I do recall "praying" in the hospital chapel the night before we turned off life support, there was no longer a real part of me that believed an embodied creator who had the power to heal him, to pull him out of his coma, back from already gone, was listening at all. I went there simply to get a reprieve from the crowded family madness of the ICU waiting room. I went for quiet, to think about my father and ponder what his loss would feel like, just as I used to when I was a child, lying in the dark of my bedroom, "practicing" I called it, for my parents' eventual death. Whatever grief I may have conjured in my imagination would feel nothing like reality.

My daughter thinks my father is in Heaven; my son thinks he is now a twenty-four-year-old person living somewhere on the planet. We joke that he's probably not our grouchy elderly cat (she's not quite old enough), but that he could potentially be one of my graduate students. When they ask me "Where is Grandpa?" I tell them the only thing I can truly believe: *He's in our hearts and our memories. He's in the stories we tell.* And I suppose I'm satisfied enough.

Paul and I talked about spirituality on our first date, in and amongst other topics like politics, art, and urban sprawl. Part of how I knew I'd become serious about him quickly was because our conversation had gotten so very serious right away. In the first years, before we married and had children, he tried to prime me on philosophy—his discipline, in which he was working on his doctorate, and of which I had almost no understanding. In a coffee shop in our college town, he explained the difference between pantheism and panentheism. Paul is exceptionally good at conveying complex ideas and theories in simple, understandable ways. And he is exceptionally patient. We're in the dining room together this morning when I ask him to re-explain the distinction.

"Well, pantheism says God *is* the cosmos—everything in creation, all life. There's no distinction between the two. Pan*en*theism says that the cosmos is *within* God; God permeates everything."

"So, in panentheism, God is distinct from the cosmos, from us?" I ask.

"Well, not exactly distinct. Let's say my toenail is the cosmos." He bends down to touch the top of his big toe. He's still in his pajamas because it's too cold to leave the house today.

"You wouldn't call my toenail distinct from me, but there's a lot more to me than my toenail."

I can't argue with that.

I'm sure he must have used a similarly charming analogy with me those years ago in the coffee house. I can't remember exactly. But the terms rattled around with me for a while, both of them appealing in their way. Months later, we lay on my bed (we had not yet moved in together), leisurely reading on a weekend morning (we had not yet had children) and I asked:

"Honey? So... are we pantheists?"

This remained a joke between us for years, first because to Paul the question seemed completely out of context (I think I was reading an article in which the term came up), but more because it seemed ridiculous to both of us that a person could ask someone else to confer upon them such a particular and private thing as a system of belief. And yet, that's exactly how I had acquired Catholicism.

My first wedding took place in a Congregational church in the town where my first husband and I went to high school. The space was spare and bright, with pale blue walls, wooden pews with crimson velvet seat cushions. A simple cross instead of baroque crucifix hanging above the altar; clear panes instead of stained glass to send light glancing off bare walls. I remember wanting simply to feel welcome. When my fiancée and I visited various Christian churches, this was the one where I felt that most keenly. The pastor, a gentle mustachioed man, took our meeting without asking a ton of questions about our background or intent. He didn't make us sign any papers or take any oaths about raising our children in a particular strain of faith. When we sat in his office, he described his congregation as being one of inclusion. "All are welcome." No hidden clause. No strings attached. We were a little smug, maybe, in our quick appraisal of the physical and spiritual space. This, we thought, is where we could belong.

Several weeks earlier, I had received a letter from a great-uncle, my grandmother's brother who was also a Franciscan friar. This was the man who married my parents, who baptized me, who gave my sister her First Holy Communion. My father, dying in the hospital, only accepted the sacrament of Last Rites because he mistook the hospital chaplain for this uncle. He was odd and funny, would take his dentures out to do bird calls and could speak both Latin and Greek. I grew up feeling fond of him.

When I was a teenager, we moved to Connecticut, and my mother invited him to bless our new home by saying Mass in our dining room. During the Prayers of the Faithful, he turned to her for help filling in the name of the local bishop, but she could not provide it. We had only lived in our new town for some months. It didn't matter. The terrible scowl on his face, the look of cold derision and dismissal let us understand what was unspoken.

In his letter to me on the eve of my wedding, though, nothing was left to interpretation. There, he used words like "fallen" and "damned" to describe me and my choice to receive this sacrament outside of his church. I learned later that he had tried to convince several family members, including my grandmother and her sisters, to boycott the wedding as he did.

I'll admit it: part of me liked the idea of this "damned"

wedding as small rebellion against my upbringing. And it wasn't my only rebellion: I was also marrying a man my father absolutely disapproved of, but his vote had been made null by his death the year before. Contrary to what my Catholic family may have felt, I did not choose a Protestant church just to hurt or offend them, just like I did not choose my first husband just to hurt or offend my father. In both cases I was mostly trying on the confidence and bravado of young adulthood.

I know now, of course, that I simplified this experience to suit my own needs, to fulfill the rebellion, to give myself permission to go through with it. I don't really know what that initial warm welcome would have grown into because we never went back to that church after our wedding day. We divorced four years later and I'm sure my uncle felt his own kind of righteous smugness then. After, I continued to treat spirituality as something of a buffet course, sampling some of this and some of that, mostly acting like a toddler at table: fickle and suspicious, unsatisfied and underfed.

The Unitarian Universalist congregation Paul and I visited before the kids were born seemed like it might be the place where I would finally feel welcome and part of something sublime. I was eight months pregnant with my atheist son when we slipped into the UU sanctuary and took seats in the back. It was August and I don't remember air conditioning. I do remember soft light through the large windows, falling over dark wood. I had no idea what to expect, really, but Paul and I were at the point I think many non-churchgoing couples get to before having children: comfortable with our own diffuse and churning (non)beliefs, but wondering if we ought to be giving something a little more solid and predictable to our kids. So, we sat down and waited for the service to begin while people smiled at us—obvious interlopers, we were too shy to make eye contact—from their own seats across the aisle. Two women walked to the front of the room (*women*—this was already a world apart!) and lit a candle set inside a metal chalice shaped like outstretched arms within a circle. Absent entirely was the

Catholic iconography of my childhood. No risen lord hanging, mangled and beatific, above a gold and white-linened altar. Simpler even than the Congregational church where I said vows the first time. There was a feeling of great openness to the room. Even while my unborn son wedged himself uncomfortably against my diaphragm, I found it easy to breathe.

We learned right away that it was customary for the summer services to be lay-led, giving the pastor a much-needed vacation. On this particular day, the focus would be on *silence* as a spiritual condition and conduit. The women talked us through a survey of various other faiths—Buddhism, I recall, and Quakerism— which include silence in their worship practices. The talk was academic and engaging and we were all asked to sit in perfect silence, "to hear our own divine voices," for the last ten minutes of the service. I felt immediately antsy. I had never been able to meditate successfully for even one minute, let alone ten, but I tried. I closed my eyes though that was not being asked of us and tried to block out the sounds of shifting chairs and bodies around me. It was all but impossible. I have a brain that does not easily quiet or turn off. I perseverate.

But Paul was sitting next to me, already calm—I could feel it—so I squeezed my eyes shut tighter and tried to regulate my breathing the way you're supposed to in yoga, which I also couldn't do very well. Soon, my very pregnant bladder would need release. Soon, I would no longer be comfortable sitting in this cushion-less chair, no matter how open and lovely the sanctuary.

I don't really know why or how—there was no great epiphany or suggestive blaze of light—but something incredible happened: I *stopped*. I stopped shifting in my seat. I stopped scrolling through my list of things we still needed to get in place for the baby. I stopped worrying that I was going to forget something crucial for his survival or ours, that I would be a poor guide for him in his life. I stopped worrying about my ability to even *be* a mother. Suddenly I was out of my head and fully into my body where a normally sedate Rudy flipped and flopped exuberantly. I sat in that silence with my hands on my belly—*on my son*—and wept in relief and, yes, in praise, for the better part of ten minutes. Similar to my old post-communion state of grace, but a hundred times more powerful, this was undeniably divine.

Sadly, I was never able to recapture this feeling with the good people of the UU because the sermon focused on something else the following week. We did attend again several more times and certainly I always felt among my tribe politically— these were progressive, pro-choice, unapologetically feminist people whose ideals matched my own and bolstered their communal practice. It should have been a perfect fit, but after the experience of our first visit, we always left feeling like we had attended a seminar rather than a spiritual coming-together. Welcome, yes, but *not belonging to*. What was missing, we said, was some deeper sense of awe.

Sister Edward Joseph did not boycott my first wedding, despite her brother, the fire and brimstone friar's entreaty. Aunt Marie, as I have always called her, is my grandmother's older sister and a Sister of Saint Joseph, a service order of Catholic nuns living in Brentwood, Long Island. This past Halloween, she turned 102 years old and the convent threw her a party complete with an enormous vanilla sheet cake with pink and yellow frosting flowers. I wasn't able to be there, but the pictures I've seen show her thin frame inside a modest habit, a wide smile on her face and light sparking from clear blue eyes.

Not only did she not boycott, she agreed to say a blessing over our marriage at the reception. I feel sure that this was not an easy thing for her to do, but she put her love for and relationship with me ahead of dogma, and not for the last time. At one point in the wedding video, the camera captures the dance floor, where at one end my ex-husband and his friends slammed into each other ecstatically inside an unlikely mosh pit, and on the other end, Aunt Marie slow danced with another uncle while Nirvana's "Smells Like Teen Spirit" played too loud on the sound system. It was a delightful moment, one that symbolizes for me her expansive spirit, and among the best things to come out of that day.

Four years later, she did not judge me for getting a divorce, and five years after *that*, did not judge me for getting remarried, once again outside of the church. She never once pressured me to baptize my children. I don't really know what was in her heart—judgment or acceptance—but I do know that each time she was faced with one of my "damned and fallen" moments, she chose to remain in my life in a loving, supportive way. Maybe she was frantically praying the rosary for my lost soul every night, but during the day, she was writing me letters about teaching French to school children, feeding the poor in soup kitchens and asking me about the daily machinations of my own life—all of this, to my mind, its own kind of prayer.

When Rudy was two years old, we had occasion to visit her convent. We arrived at the beautiful green grounds in mid-August and took her out to lunch at Friendly's where we ordered hamburgers and milkshakes. Rudy scribbled with crayons on the paper placemats and Aunt Marie took to engaging Paul in a conversation about the theologian Saint Thomas Aquinas. I don't remember the content of what they talked about, but I do remember the quality of intellectual curiosity and genuine interest. This sort of gesture was typical of Sister Edward Joseph: she thought deeply about the person in front of her—in this case, an academic philosopher—and worked to find a place of mutual respect and exchange.

Back at the convent, as we strolled from the car to her quarters, I noticed she was walking with a gingerly step.

"Aunt Marie?" I asked taking her by the elbow. "Are you okay?"

"Oh, yes dear, just fine. Though I did take a bit of a tumble last week. It was the loveliest evening and I was walking back from chapel, looking up at the heavens. When I reached the main house, I punched my code into the keypad for entry just like always, but then I got distracted by this one star that was glowing even more brightly than the others. Glorious! And as I stood there pondering whether it was a star at all—perhaps it was actually Mars?—the heavy door swung closed and knocked me down."

Before he dedicated himself to philosophy, Paul thought he

might want to study Physics. He had grown up watching and loving Carl Sagan's PBS series, "Cosmos," drawn to the tension and interplay between the observable universe and that which remains ineffable all around us. I think both my husband and my great-aunt would agree with Sagan when he said, "Science is not only compatible with spirituality; it is a profound source of spirituality." Apparently, this kind of thinking, this comfort with ambiguity, a belief in both/and, is in our blood. I hope my son, too, will someday come to allow his reason to lie flat on its back, face up under a summer night sky dazzling with awe.

At the end of this past fall semester, I invited my creative writing class to our home for a potluck dinner and a final reading of the work they had written for their portfolios. They arrived by ones and twos, bearing bottles of wine, casseroles, brownies and other nibbles. One brought a Turkish bread he had baked in a home-built oven. "It didn't really rise," he apologized, "but next time I'll get it right." The doorbell rang again. It was my Tibetan student, K., and a woman she had asked if she could bring along as a guest. I took their coats and asked,

"So, how do you know K.?"

"Oh, I work in the kitchen in the dorms up there," she explained. "We've gotten pretty close. I keep my eye on her."

K. came to Pittsburgh to study with us under a program sponsored by the Indian government. Though she was born and raised there, she is actually the daughter of Tibetan refugees and has never been to her own home country. I remember reading her personal essay and writing sample before she was admitted and noting that her story—one of identity and diaspora—was raw with longing. She'd been having a hard time acclimating to being so far from home and in such an unfamiliar culture and landscape. I was worried about her.

"I'm so glad you're here," I told her, meaning my living room. "And I'm so glad you're here for K. Thank you."

We milled around and built our dinners from the many plates on the table. The students talked about their final papers in other classes and about their plans for the winter break. I knew that K. would not be going back to India to see her family, but back up to the dorms on our northern campus, 45 minutes away. It seemed like a lonely way to spend three weeks. "At least she'll have her friend there," I thought.

I went into the kitchen to grab napkins and plates and K. followed me.

"I was so surprised to see the flags," she said, gesturing back towards the front porch where we have hung traditional Tibetan prayer flags from the hooks where the ferns hang in the summer. The idea of breeze-blown blessings—the earth itself praying for all of us—fills me with such calm. K's expression was neutral, not smiling but not pinched or pained either. I felt myself flush a little and realized I wasn't sure how to answer her. Had I offended her? Had I made her feel further displaced? Unwelcome? Did she think the Buddha on our mantel was simply decorative? Was it?

In the end I didn't explain the flags or that the mandala hanging above the fireplace was a family heirloom brought back from Paul's grandparents' travels in Nepal. I didn't tell the story about how, when Paul and I decided to get married, I found my wedding dress—a deep green, sleeveless silk shantung with a subtle bustle in the back—while browsing in a Tibetan store in Greenwich Village. I had gone in to look at the jewelry while Paul was looking at records or books down the street, and found, in the back of the store, a rack of garments. I knew I wanted to wear a green dress this time—I had been looking online for several weeks—and there it was. I tried it on and it was perfect. Beautiful. Paul wandered back and joined me at the counter where I was telling the proprietor that I would be wearing this dress to my own wedding. I had my credit card out when he said, "Wait!" and walked across the store to a shelf lined with colorful fabrics. When he returned, he was holding two lengths of white silk.

"These are called *katas*," he told us. "In Tibetan Buddhism we use them to mark auspicious occasions. I would like to give these to you. A gift. It means I will pray for you for the rest of my life."

A few months later, at the end of May, we used the silks for a ritual we created, in a wedding ceremony we wrote ourselves, which was blessed by a Unitarian minister who felt comfortable presiding over our spiritual hodgepodge. We had hired her specifically because she was taking a symbolic stand by refusing to marry straight couples until she could also marry gay ones. Those good progressive Unitarians. Our tribe. "Sign us up!" we said and had a justice of the peace make us legal earlier that day.

I remember that I had hesitated for a moment to take those *katas* from the shopkeeper, that word "co-option" ringing like a brass bell in my head. But it was only for a moment. Bright silver baubles and chunky turquoise and lapis gems gleamed from the glass cabinets and the air over-spilled with the spice of incense—sandalwood here, instead of frankincense—but I knew I was in a holy space. I was inside of a holy moment. I believed it when he said he would pray for us.

We haven't been back to the Hindu temple in Monroeville, nor have we visited the Dharma center in Oakland yet, but we'd like to. Or maybe the Quaker meeting in Shadyside where we can dwell for a little while in that devotional silence that had so moved me when I was still on the cusp of my new life and self as mother, and which is principle to their practice of worship. We had made our way to the Quaker meeting in our old town precisely *because* we longed to recapture that profound experience of silence the UU's had given us a first taste of.

When we attended the State College Friends meeting (we never did become members), the kids were too little to sit still, let alone still *and* silent, so Paul and I split the meeting time so that one of us would play with the kids outside while the other sat in the sanctuary. Then we would switch. In Quakerism, the idea is that you try to listen for the "still, small voice" of the divine (yes, you could call it God, though Quakers don't insist upon it) to speak to and through you. One Sunday when the kids were small and exhausting, I was ready, the way all parents are, to have *just five minutes of peace and quiet, for the love of God!* I needed a space to clear my head. It was my turn. With the windows open to the soft spring morning, I closed my eyes.

Cardinals came first. We call them "Rudy birds" because of their song, "Ru-DEE, Ru-DEE."

Then, a bumblebee. More bird call.

Wind through trees.

Paul's voice. Josephine squealing.

The swish and clang of the swing set.

My own blood flow.

My breath. Slow and deep, in and out.

I listened.

I'm still listening.

ON CRYING

For most of my life, I was terrified to sing out loud. I thought—
no, *I knew*—I had a terrible voice. My mother couldn't carry a
tune, and I was sure I was just like her. She sang to me often as
a child, but instead of soothing me, as was certainly her inten-
tion, it made me uncomfortable. Her lullabies were Irish rebel
songs, dirges about doomed men in damp prisons, awaiting
their deaths by hanging in the morning, but that wasn't the
most uncomfortable part. It was her delivery. She had a low,
raspy smoker's voice and would sort of speak-sing them. I can
remember cringing to hear the unnatural drop off at the end of
a phrase, the way students sometimes read poems, followed by
a quick, short intake of breath before starting the next. Like a
hiccup or a gasp for more air. A clipping of wings for birds that
should soar. Later, she'd let her erratic lead foot push the car to
accelerate, then take it off and let it glide until she needed more
speed. Down, up, and then back to the floor. These were the
days of too much to drink. Of choosing between two bottles of
red wine before bed, or else crying herself to sleep after her
marriage to my father disintegrated and then he died. The years
of her driving her car onto neighbor's lawns, somehow not
killing herself or someone else. For a long time, we swam away
from each other on opposite currents. But when my kids were
born, she got sober and we floated back to one another. It was

more complicated than that, but it was enough. She died of lung cancer nine months ago.

In the 80s and early 90s when she was a rising and then established star, I wasn't really aware of the music of Canadian Country singer, k.d. lang. I was busy being a fawning girlfriend, and the voiceless wife, to a swaggering smart guy, who turned off whatever I happened to be listening to and blasted, instead, Metallica and Ministry from the flimsy speakers in the brown, drab living room of our sad, drab duplex in Naugatuck, Connecticut. After he left me—an utter obliteration—I worked as a nanny for a lesbian couple whose kids loved me, who became my family, who, in my mother's absence, helped me put myself back together. I would do their laundry sometimes, folding soft linen shirts and skirts into piles on the dining room table, and wonder who I was. I had just started feeling drawn to women's bodies. Their hips, ample like my own, I found especially distracting. Later, a lesbian grad school professor of mine would say "like attracts like," as an explanation for why she always fell for swaggering, smart Butches. I ask you, in the 80's and 90s, was there a more famous Butch lesbian musician than k.d. lang?

Before my thirties, there is only one time I sang intentionally, by myself, in front of other people. It was 1988 and I was auditioning for the part of Glinda the Good Witch in my high school's production of *The Wizard of Oz*. I sang two or three verses of "Somewhere Over the Rainbow" into the awful spotlight of the mostly empty auditorium, knowing my teachers and classmates were looking at me, and worse, listening to me. I felt like I would faint or throw up. After, an ex-boyfriend who was a musician, approached me and said, "I didn't know you could sing." I didn't believe him. I was sure he had misheard me.

. . .

In 1988, k.d. lang appeared on stage on the program *Top of the Pops* with Rock legend, Roy Orbison, to perform his 1961 hit, "Crying." Having heard her early work and been impressed, Orbison invited the twenty-seven-year-old lang to record a duet of the song the previous year, thus securing her status as both icon and iconoclast in the Country and Pop music landscape for at least the next decade.

For me, the decade that followed my terrifying live audition (I didn't land the part of Glinda but was instead cast as Munchkin Number 2. I declined.), included a marriage, a divorce, a graduate degree, and a reinvention of myself. I wouldn't go so far to say *iconoclast* here, but I did what I could to undo many of the things I had once believed in for and about myself. I pawned my diamond engagement ring for almost no money and loved the dark symbolism of that. I dropped my wedding dress off at a Goodwill in New Haven. I fought a judge for over a year to get my last name back. I became a feminist. I got a tattoo. I kissed the lips of a girl with hips like mine.

Roy Orbison had an angel's voice. Routinely, when we listen to his music at home, my husband and I marvel at the clarity of the tone, the smooth, delicious, pitch-perfect richness of that great man's talent. If you've ever watched videos of Orbison singing, you know that even when he hits those highest, most out-of-the-reach-of-mortals notes, his face shows no strain. He simply opens his mouth, and the notes soar out and up, up as if on the wing. He was an astonishing, singular talent, that is not to be denied. And "Crying" is as classic a song as we have in our American songbook. It's a ballad of love and lament for what's been lost. Imagine you are a person who runs into an old love, someone who has left and gone on to make a new life, maybe with someone new. You exchange pleasantries—*hello, how are you, it's been so long*—and you think, with relief, *okay, I got this. I am over this person.* It doesn't hurt anymore. Or, at least, it doesn't hurt the same. And then, in parting, you find your hand held tightly in friendship and well wishes and nostalgia and goodbye, and suddenly it all falls apart and you find yourself crying. Alone and crying.

Science calls this phenomenon *frisson*. It's basically a physical reaction to intense stimuli—emotional feeling or experience. It's the same autonomic nervous response as what happens when we get goose bumps or chills from the touch of someone we love or find sexually attractive. A spark in the skin that ignites a dopamine fire. Frisson is also sometimes referred to as a "skin orgasm" because of the waves of pleasure that wash over the person experiencing it.

If you've ever felt chills while looking at visual art or listening to music, then you've experienced frisson. Not everyone does. Some studies suggest as few as 50% of us have nervous systems wired for it. I'm one of the lucky people who do, given the right music, the right voice. Here are some songs that elicit frisson in me: "Don't Fear the Reaper," by Blue Oyster Cult, "Oh Holy Night," the traditional Christmas hymn, "Stairway to Heaven" by Led Zeppelin but only as performed by Ann Wilson of Heart at the Kennedy Center, "When Doves Cry," by Prince, and Roy Orbison's "Crying" as performed by k.d. lang.

After listening to lang sing "Crying" a bunch of times for this essay, and experiencing those waves of pleasure, I wondered if I would have the same reaction to hearing Orbison's version. I feel certain that his voice has elicited this response in me in the past, but I wasn't sure. I had to test it. So, I conducted a Very Scientific Experiment. The table below presents data that tracks my heart rate (I wore my Apple watch) and tallies the number of chills I got while listening to the same song sung by the two vocalists. My method: listen to three different recordings by Orbison, followed by the famous Orbison/lang duet, and then three different recordings by lang, all of which I found on YouTube. I kept my eyes closed during the listening so that my data wouldn't be skewed by visual stimuli.

An Analysis of the Effects of "Crying" on Sheila's Autonomic Nervous System

Pittsburgh, Pennsylvania, January 2022

ARTIST	PERFORMANCE	STARTING HR	ENDING HR	# OF CHILLS
Roy Orbison	Original studio recording	100	80	0
Roy Orbison	Monument Concert, 1965	90	91	.5
Roy Orbison	Black and White Night 30	89	90	1
Roy Orbison & k.d. lang	Top of the Pops, 1988	90	91	6
k.d. lang	MTV Unplugged, 1993	92	81	13
k.d. lang	Kennedy Center Tribute, 1990	81	96	16
k.d. lang	Roy Orbison Tribute, I couldn't find a date for this one. She looks a little older, though. Early 2000s?	91	91	11

The results surprised me. I would have expected Orbison to rate higher, and even though I wasn't shocked to see lang pull it out as clear winner in terms of quantity of chills given, I really thought MTV's stripped-down version would come out ahead of the Kennedy center's more orchestral performance, because I really don't love all that over production. But then again, it might be the very presence of that sweeping instrumentation that gave it the edge. According to the article "Have You Ever had a Skin Orgasm" by Ainsley Hawthorne, PhD in *Psychology Today*, "the features that most commonly induce frisson are ones that violate our expectations, like crescendos, the onset of unexpected harmonies, the entrance of the human voice or affecting lyrics." So, maybe flutes, too? I don't know what's going on with my heart rate here, because many times I could feel my face blush while listening, but the numbers didn't show an appreciable increase. Though interestingly it looks like where lang's Kennedy Center "Crying" puts me into a state of clear ecstasy, Orbison's studio version calms me down. I should also note that I listened to these in the sequence they appear here, and with no down time in between, so that by the time I got to the final version, I was having the odd sensation of feeling like the chills were there, but I couldn't *quite* feel them. Like they were dulled by... overuse? How many times can one experience this sort of euphoria before becoming a little spent?

Well, this has gotten steamier than I expected it to at the start of my little experiment. Let's leave it at this: 1990s lang, with her sharp suits and sharper jaw, close-cropped hair, skin like moonlight, and, *oh yes*, swagger, looks nothing like me, but frisson doesn't lie. The hypothalamus wants what it wants.

Alcohol abuse damages several parts of the brain including the cerebellum—which is responsible for the motor coordination and reflex action that would have helped my mother not drive her car onto a neighbor's lawn—and the limbic system, which controls our emotions. At my mother's (fully vaxxed) memorial at the Jersey Shore this past summer, we, her daughters, sat under a canopy among her many brothers, cousins, nephews, nieces, and grandchildren. That is to say, my children. The past year of anticipating a death that was hard on all of us, was hardest of all on my daughter who had an especially close relationship with my mother. When my daughter was born my mother got sober, finally, and for good. That was fourteen years ago. Fourteen years of healing and largely normal, healthy (if not always positive), emotional response. My daughter studies voice at a performing arts high school here in Pittsburgh. She is a Singer. She loves to be in the spotlight, on the stage. This is her identity in the same way that I am a Writer. When she saw my mother's casket at the church, she let out an involuntary wail that shook every heart in that building. I wailed too, but quietly, into my husband's shoulder, into myself. She opened her throat and screamed her pain out. After the service, under the canopy, my mother's cousins gently cared for my daughter. They held and rocked her and told her how much she is loved. They asked her to sing, so she stood in the center and sang "Edelweiss" from *The Sound of Music.* We all cried. How could you not? I had gone to get a piece of cake and talk to a cousin, when behind me, under the same canopy, another powerful voice erupted in a different song,

"In a dreary Brixton prison / where an Irish rebel lay..."

and I stood, mute with shock, and listened. These were the words to the dirge, the lullaby my mother would sing to me as a small child, the one that filled me with discomfort and embarrassment for her, and caused me to silence my own song for much of my life. I had never head them sung by anyone else.

"By his side a priest was standing / 'ere his soul should pass away..."

My mother's older brother, Tommy, sang "Shall My Soul Pass Through Old Ireland" with sad, clear tones that lifted and soared up, up through the top of the canopy, and out over the Atlantic Ocean, and I cried and felt love and shame and regret and relief for the fourteen years we had.

In grad school, in Kim's kitchen, we cooked tuna burgers out of a Martha Stuart cookbook and laughed at how outrageously expensive they were. Chaka Khan spun in the CD player and we sang along. In her car, on the way to somewhere, we had the windows down and the Indigo Girls on. I must have forgotten myself, the way you can with great music, because I still, at this point in early 2000s, only let myself hum along to songs when I was with other people. I still felt embarrassed about my voice. I skipped out on karaoke night every time. I only know I was actually singing in the car because I got all tied into knots trying to navigate the sonic complexity of those songs, trying, as one does, to sing both melody and harmony *at the same time*, and ended up laughing and saying something like, "Oh god that was awful. I can't sing!" And then Kim, who has a beautiful singing voice, said the thing that changed my self-perception for the rest of my life: "Of course you can. You have a voice like k.d. lang's."

I knew my friend did not mean that I could *sing* like k.d. lang. She meant that, like, lang, my voice sounds comfortable in the lower range. Lang is actually a mezzo-soprano—as is my daughter—but I cannot hit those high notes.

Five years after this moment in the car with my friend who
had no idea the gift she had just given me—the damage she'd
just undone—I would find myself in a darkened nursery, rocking
my infant son to sleep, singing "Here Comes the Sun," singing,
"Rudi Can't Fail," singing, as I would also to my daughter two
years later, every verse of "Somewhere Over the Rainbow,"
brightly and with something close to confidence, but also *dolce*,
dolce, so as not to wake them, as mothers do.

The month before she died, I sat next to my mother on the
white leather couch in her southern Florida living room. Cancer
had made her so small she had almost disappeared, and she
knew she was going to die very soon. She told me she was ready
for it. We had spent several weeks over Zoom together earlier
in the year, before she lost so much of her cognition. "I want
you to interview me about my life," she said. "I have some
things I want to say." So, we moved through her seventy years,
one decade at a time. I felt anxious as we approached the 1990s
—those were some of my darkest years. My father died. My
marriage died. My relationship with my mother ached from the
strain of her alcoholism, my resentment and our total misunder-
standing of each other as people. What would she say about all
of that? What would I?

It turned out, we said nothing about those most defining
moments of my life. Her memories of the 90s looked different.
They were filled with the stuff of *her* life and that's what she
wanted to talk about. It made sense, finally. We were, and
always had been, separate people whose lives intersected irregu-
larly. This sounds lonely, but I don't mean it to. Maybe it's how
mothers and daughters should be after a time. Both of us
moving forward on our own journey, both stranger and familiar
to one another, waving and smiling as we pass on the way.

She was done talking now. Tired, often confused and already
beginning to transition to the next realm. I pulled out my
phone and opened YouTube. I wanted to make things easier for
her. Softer. I thought we'd listen to some music to pass the
time, so I cued up Simon and Garfunkel, a favorite of hers for

my whole life. "Mrs. Robinson" played from my tinny phone speaker and I started to sing to my mother, and my mother sang every word with me. An unexpected harmony. I cried, knowing that soon I would lose her, that I'd be standing alone, as we all do, in my grief. I cried. I'm still crying.

But I'm so glad we sang.

GRATITUDE

I am grateful to the editors of these publications, which published the following essays in this collection:

"Bodies of Saltwater," *Appalachian Literature*
"Self-Portrait with Rollercoaster," *Barrelhouse*
"Four Menus," *Brevity*
"Rocky's Manicotti," *The Inquisitive Eater*
"Cry, Baby," "The Eyes Have It," "All Things Edible, Random and Odd, "*Literary Mama*
"Pin the Solje on the Baby," *PANK*
"Pruning the Fern," *Phoebe*
"Turtle Soup," *Potomac Review*
"Tornado," *River Teeth*
"After the Verdict We Watch Fireworks," "Strip District Meats," *The Rumpus*
"The Greenland Shark," *Signal Mountain Review*
"Meat Ragu," *Sweet: A Literary Confection*
"Mock Turtle Soup," *Under the Gum Tree*
"Dead Dad Day," *Waccamaw*

"Mixtape for a Too-Young Marriage" appeared in the anthology *Come as You Are*
"On Crying," made it through round 1 of the March X-ness essay tournament on Twitter, 2022

I began writing the essays in this collection in 2004. Back then, I imagined it would be a memoir strictly about my the loss of my father and our relationship through food, but as time passed and life changed—deepening in complexity as it does when one adds a marriage, a divorce, another marriage, children, a career, the ephemera of years—it, did, too. Because the book covers so much time, it includes many characters (some whose names I've changed because that's the kind thing to do), and they are bound up with many different moments of my life. Some of those moments were hard when I experienced them and remain hard in memory and writing. Some were hard then but have long since softened. Or, I have. Some of the people herein have been gone from my life for a long while and some are still present in various ways. I want to say to all of them, *thank you.* You gave me a lot to live through and grow from and great material for writing!

I want to acknowledge the people who were there at the beginning of my life as a memoirist: my MFA pals who trauma-bonded with me through V.G.'s memoir workshop—Kim, Jenn, Danielle, Liz, Aimee and Bob. We survived her! I will always be grateful to *Glamour Magazine*, whose "Story of Your Life" contest helped me define a totally new writerly self. Thank you to Caroline Grant who affirmed me and my writing early and often, and Dave Housley, friend, cheerleader, helpful problem-solver. How I miss our Wegmans lunches! Cindy Clem Speigel and Sandra Faulkner read early versions of this book and offered feedback and encouragement over the years, and I love them both dearly for that and for many other reasons.

Parts of this book were written during residencies at the MacDowell Colony and the Virginia Center for the Creative Arts and I'm grateful for the time and space I was afforded in those communities.

Because the writing of this book spans the entirety of my professional life, I feel gratitude to both of my institutions—Penn State University and Chatham University—for giving me a way to support myself and my family as a writer and a teacher, and to my colleagues in Burrowes Building and Lindsay House, particularly Julia Spicher Kasdorf and Anissa Wardi for so many good, chewy conversations about motherhood that made me feel less alone.

I am grateful for the support of the Pittsburgh literary

community, which has provided me with cherished friendships and professional opportunities in abundance.

Thank you forever to my kick-ass therapist, Max, whose support and guidance these past ten years helped me grow professionally, raise my kids, strengthen my marriage and deepen my relationship with the writer and artist I am still becoming.

Thank you to CLASH Books, to Leza and Christoph, for their great enthusiasm about this book and the care they have taken to bring it into the world.

Finally, I thank my family—my father who didn't live long enough to see me become a published writer and my mother who showed up to a Zoom reading of mine while she was going through chemotherapy in the last months of her life. I miss you. I hope you are both proud of me and this work. Thanks to my sister Catherine who once hand wrote the words to a poem of mine all over the bathroom walls in her house. I still can't believe you did that. I love you, freak.

Thank you to Rudy and Josephine, my spectacular children whose lives are documented *with their permission* in these pages. I hope if/when you read it, you will feel I treated you honestly, with admiration, respect and deepest love. You are my world.

And to Paul, for accepting and loving every iteration of me —past, present, future. It's not easy, I would imagine, to be an introvert married to a memoirist. Thanks for kimchi and pantheism and forgiving me for reading that one thing in public early on and for sticking around for these twenty years. I'm so happy I found you on the internet and clicked "add to cart!" 152H.

ABOUT THE AUTHOR

SHEILA SQUILLANTE is a poet and essayist living in Pittsburgh. She is the author of the poetry collections, *Mostly Human*, winner of the 2020 Wicked Woman Book Prize from BrickHouse Books, and *Beautiful Nerve*, (Tiny Hardcore Books, 2015) as well as four chapbooks of poetry: *Dear Sunder, In This Dream of My Father, Women Who Pawn Their Jewelry* and *A Woman Traces the Shoreline*. She directs and teaches in the MFA program at Chatham University where she serves as Executive Editor of *The Fourth River,* a journal of nature and place-based writing. She is also an Editor-at-Large for *Barrelhouse* Magazine, an unlikely bulldog lover and an abstract visual artist. During the pandemic she ripped out her front lawn and planted a garden.

ALSO BY CLASH BOOKS

AFTERWORD
Nina Schuyler

PROXIMITY
Sam Heaps

GAG REFLEX
Elle Nash

BORN TO BE PUBLIC
Greg Mania

DELICIOUS DISHES FOR YOU & YOUR DOG
Lisa Goddard

WHAT ARE YOU
Lindsay Lerman

GAG REFLEX
Elle Nash

SEPARATION ANXIETY
Janice Lee

THE BEE & THE FLY:
THE IMPROBABLE CORRESPONDENCE
OF LOUISA MAY ALCOTT & EMILY DICKINSON
Lorraine Tosiello & Jane Cavolita

BAD FOUNDATIONS
Brian Allen Carr

WE PUT THE LIT IN LITERARY

CLASHBOOKS.COM

FOLLOW US
FB
TWITTER
IG
@clashbooks

Printed in the USA
CPSIA information can be obtained
at www.ICGtesting.com
JSHW020937241123
52664JS00004B/57